Promoting Effective Group
Work in the Primary Classroom

D0239342

LIVERPOOL
JOHN MOORES UNIVERSITY
I.M. MARSH LIBRARY
BARKHILL ROAD
LIVERPOOL L17 6BD
TEL. 0151 231 5216/5299

LIVERPOOL JMU LIBRARY

3 1111 01294 0191

TLRP Improving Practice Series

Series Editor: Director of the ESRC Teaching and Learning Programme.

Learning How to Learn: Tools for Schools
Mary James *et al.*

Improving Primary Literacy: Linking Home and School
Martin Hughes *et al.*

Improving Primary Mathematics: Linking Home and School (forthcoming)
Martin Hughes *et al.*

Thinking Lessons for Thinking Classrooms: Tools for Teachers
Carol McGuinness *et al.*

Promoting Effective Group Work in the Primary Classroom

A handbook for teachers and practitioners

Ed Baines, Peter Blatchford and Peter Kutnick

with Anne Chowne, Cathy Ota and Lucia Berdondini

Routledge
Taylor & Francis Group

LONDON AND NEW YORK

First published 2009
by Routledge
2 Park Square, Milton Park, Abingdon, Oxon, OX14 4RN

Simultaneously published in the USA and Canada
by Routledge
270 Madison Avenue, NY 10016

Routledge is an imprint of the Taylor & Francis Group, an informa business

© 2009 Ed Baines, Peter Blatchford and Peter Kutnick

Typeset in Melior and Futura by
Keystroke, 28 High Street, Tettenhall, Wolverhampton
Printed and bound in Great Britain by
MPG Books Ltd, Bodmin

All rights reserved. No part of this book may be reprinted or reproduced or utilised
in any form or by any electronic, mechanical, or other means, now known or
hereafter invented, including photocopying and recording, or in any information
storage or retrieval system, without permission in writing from the publishers.

British Library Cataloguing in Publication Data
A catalogue record for this book is available from the British Library

Library of Congress Cataloging-in-Publication Data
Promoting effective group work in the primary classroom: a handbook for teachers
and practitioners/Ed Baines . . . [et al.].
        p. cm. — (Improving practice)
    Includes index.
    1. Group work in education—Handbooks, manuals, etc.   I. Baines, Ed, 1969-
LB1032.P77 2008
    371.39′5—dc22   2008003039

ISBN 10: 0-415-41687-6

ISBN 13: 978-0-415-41687-0

Contents

Series preface

The ideas for *Improving Practice* contained in this book are underpinned by high-quality research from the Teaching and Learning Research Programme (TLRP), the UK's largest ever coordinated investment in education enquiry. Each suggestion has been tried and tested with experienced practitioners and has been found to improve learning outcomes – particularly if the underlying principles about Teaching and Learning have been understood. The key, then, remains the exercise of professional judgement, knowledge and skill. We hope that the *Improving Practice* series will encourage and support teachers in exploring new ways of enhancing learning experiences and improving educational outcomes of all sorts. For future information about TLRP, and additional 'practitioner applications', see www.tlrp.org.

Acknowledgements

The SPR*in*G (Social Pedagogic Research into Group work) project was a four-year project funded by the Economic and Social Research Council (www.esrc.ac. uk) as part of the Teaching and Learning Research Programme (www.tlrp.org). The production of this handbook for primary schools is the result of a collaborative effort between teachers and researchers based at the Institute of Education, University of Brighton and King's College, London.

Chapter 1

Background to the handbook

Introduction

This handbook is the result of a four-year study that brought together teachers and researchers in the exploration of how pupil group work can be made more effective in support of children's learning. The research study, known as the 'SPRinG' project, developed and evaluated a new approach to group work in primary schools. It was funded by the Economic and Social Research Council's Teaching and Learning Research Programme. SPRinG is an acronym for Social Pedagogic Research into Group work, and is based upon the view that effective group work can be facilitated through:

1 Careful attention to the physical and social organisation of the classroom and groups.
2 The development of pupils' group-working skills (based upon an inclusive relational approach, working with *all* children in a class).
3 The creation and structuring of challenging tasks that legitimise group work.
4 The supportive involvement of teachers and other adults.

The project had two aims: first, to work with teachers to develop strategies which would enhance the quality of group and paired work; and, second, to evaluate whether these strategies would result in an improvement in pupils' attainment and learning, behaviour and attitudes to school. The project evaluation involved 162 classes in primary and secondary schools, and 4,259 pupils aged 5 to 14. This handbook focuses only on children in primary schools.

Findings showed that engaging in the SPRinG group-work programme had a positive effect on all pupils. Group work led to gains in attainment and learning, greater levels of active classroom engagement and discussions, and a reassurance among pupils and teachers that working in groups was a positive classroom experience.

What makes SPRinG distinctive?

The SPRinG approach applies group work across the curriculum and over the school year. We worked with teachers to develop a programme that could be successfully integrated into school life and the curriculum, and that recognised the concerns and difficulties teachers can have with group work. This collaboration between researchers and teachers extended for two years or more. Each class was expected to undertake at least two one-hour SPRinG group-work sessions per week.

A strength of the SPRinG programme is that it is based on a long-term systematic evaluation of pupil progress over a full school year and comparison with a control group in terms of objective measures of attainment and classroom behaviour.

What did we find?

Key finding 1

Far from impeding learning, group work raised levels of achievement. In the early years of primary school, group work helped to improve attainment in reading and mathematics. SPR*in*G activities for older primary school pupils were targeted at science and led to significantly higher attainment and deeper conceptual understanding and inferential thinking.

Key finding 2

Despite some teachers' worries that group work might be disruptive, pupil behaviour *improved* in the SPR*in*G classes. Children were able to take more responsibility for their own behaviour and learning, freeing up teacher time to observe and reflect upon classroom activities.

Key finding 3

Group work doubled pupils' levels of sustained, active engagement in learning and more than doubled the amount of high-level, thoughtful discussion between children.

Other findings

- Teachers' professional skills and confidence were enhanced and their teaching repertoire was extended. There were also unexpected benefits – for example, as pupils developed group-working skills, teachers found they were 'freed' from classroom control and were able to spend more time teaching.
- Group work seemed to be most effective when adopted by the whole school, rather than individual teachers.
- Teachers working in areas of deprivation or in difficult circumstances found that group work could be used successfully and can aid classroom relationships and social inclusion.

Further information

Further details of the findings of this research can be found at www.spring-project.org.uk or www.tlrp.org and from the following published articles and reports:

Baines, E., Blatchford, P. and Kutnick, P. (2008) Pupil grouping for learning: developing a social pedagogy of the classroom, in R. Gillies, A. Ashman and J. Terwel (eds) *The Teacher's Role in Implementing Cooperative Learning in the Classroom*, New York: Springer-Verlag.

Baines, E., Blatchford, P. and Chowne, A. (2007) Improving the effectiveness of collaborative group work in primary schools: effects on Science attainment. ESRC Teaching and Learning Research Programme special issue of the *British Educational Research Journal*, 33.

Blatchford, P., Baines, E., Rubie-Davies, C., Bassett, P. and Chowne, A. (2006) The effect of a new approach to group work on pupil–pupil and teacher–pupil interactions. *Journal of Educational Psychology*, 98, 750–65.

Blatchford, P., Baines, E., Kutnick, P. and Galton, M. (2005) Improving pupil group work in classrooms: A new approach to increasing engagement and learning in everyday classroom settings at Key Stages 1, 2 and 3. *ESRC TLRP Research Briefing 11, Nov 2005*. ISBN 0-85473-730-8 (available from www.tlrp.org).

Blatchford, P., Galton, M., Kutnick, P., and Baines, E. (2005) *Improving the effectiveness of pupil groups in classrooms*. Final Report to ESRC (Ref: L139 25 1046).

Kutnick, P., Ota, C. and Berdondini, L. (2008). Improving the effects of group working in classrooms with young school-aged children: Facilitating attainment, interaction and classroom activity, *Learning and Instruction*, 18, 83–95.

The SPR*in*G programme

The practices and recommended activities in the handbook are based upon the collective wisdom of collaborating teachers and researchers, previous research, and the results of the SPR*in*G study. The SPR*in*G programme is based on four key principles for successful group work:

- The classroom and pupil groups need to be strategically organised and managed. Attention to classroom-seating arrangements and the characteristics of groups – such as their size, composition and stability – over time can make group work more effective.
- Group-work skills have to be developed. We cannot just put children into groups and expect them to work well together. Based on a 'relational approach' that encourages children to want to work together, activities in the handbook are designed to help pupils trust and respect each other; communicate effectively through listening, explaining and sharing ideas; and plan, organise and evaluate their group work.
- Group-work activities should encourage group work. Careful attention to the nature and structure of activities can ensure that group work is productive.
- Adults should adopt a range of roles that are supportive of group work and that encourage pupil independence rather than teaching pupils directly.

Getting children to work together is not easy and requires perseverance, reflection, problem-solving and a host of other skills on the part of both the teacher and pupils. The positive aspects of effective group work take time and planning. They certainly are not learned over night and it may take some time before you notice a clear change in the capabilities of your pupils. However, the rewards reported by many teachers and our findings concerning pupil development are worthy of the effort that is invested. Group work offers learning possibilities for pupils not provided by either teacher-led or individual work, and can help to improve attitudes to work and classroom behaviour. We hope that this handbook will lead to more systematic use of group work. It deserves to be given a more central role in educational policy and school practice.

Structure of this handbook

The handbook is composed of two parts: the first provides recommendations and information about how group work can be successfully used and implemented in primary school classrooms; the second provides examples of a developmental programme of activities.

In Chapter 2 we outline the case for group work, providing an explanation as to why it can be a powerful learning context and information on how best to implement it. Chapter 3 encourages teachers to reflect on how their classrooms are currently organised and the success of group work in their classes. Chapters 4 to 7 provide details of each of the key principles and the recommended practices for improving the effectiveness of group work and pupils' group-work skills. Chapter 8 provides suggestions and tools to help teachers and pupils reflect on and evaluate group work. Working from simple forms of group work to more complex group projects, Chapter 9 provides suggestions on how to start utilising group work in the curriculum.

Chapter 10 offers a range of useful ideas for overcoming common difficulties with group work.

The units in Part II provide a selection of group-work training activities designed to develop pupils' social, communication and advanced group-work skills. These activities are organised into a developmental sequence that aims to build up group-working skills incrementally. These activities can be supplemented with your own ideas.

Part I

Developing group work in your classroom

Chapter 2

Introduction

The case for group work

One of the most important aspects of growing up is learning how to interact and work with others. The skills involved are used in our everyday social interactions with others, at work and at home. But the skills that underpin group work (what we refer to as group-working skills) are often taken for granted and assumed to develop fairly naturally through our everyday interactions with family, friends and acquaintances.

In school, children are often told how they should and should not behave and work. But they are rarely given the opportunity to learn how to interact and work with others or to reflect on these interactions and their interpersonal skills. Some of the skills involved can be socially and/or intellectually complex: for example, sustaining a discussion on a topic, explaining reasoning, helping others without over-helping, developing an argument or counter-argument, reaching a consensus or compromise, bringing others into the discussion, planning group work and so on. It is important that teachers and schools provide opportunities for children to learn these essential social skills so that they can gain more from future learning opportunities and take a more active role in their own learning in the future.

We also know that in any classroom there are three main learning contexts. First, there are those involving interactions between the teacher and pupils in the class. Second, there are those when children are working on their own on a task. The third is when children are working with each other. We know from research in primary and secondary schools that children spend much of their time either listening to the teacher or working on their own, but it is unlikely that you will see children working together on a task. They can be seated in groups, of course, but they are not often working together *as* a group. On the other hand, children spend much more classroom time in the presence of their peers than with a teacher or working on their own.

When groups are organised in classrooms this is often in the interest of classroom management, ability differentiation and in response to the classroom layout. There is little sign of a pedagogic relationship between features of groupings, such as group size, and learning purposes or the nature of the task set. Research has also shown that teachers have little faith in pupils' ability to work in groups, and pupils rarely have the skills to prepare themselves for group work. There is a cycle at work in that teachers' beliefs are consistent with the difficulties they encounter with group work, while pupils' behaviour in groups and lack of success in turn confirms some teachers' belief that group work is of little value.

It is our view that effective group work does not receive the recognition it deserves and hardly figures in educational policies for primary schools. When used well, group work can enhance pupils' learning, motivation and ability to work together, and can encourage children to be less dependent on the teacher by taking more responsibility for their own behaviour and learning.

What is group work?

There is more to group work than sitting pupils in groups and asking them to work together. By group work we mean just that – pupils working together as a group or team for a joint purpose or outcome. The children may work on a practical task, on a problem that requires one solution, brainstorming or discussing views on a local issue about which views are strong. We argue that group work can be used across all curriculum areas, and for many different types of task. In this handbook our emphasis is on developing group-work skills that support learning and, in particular, activities that encourage high-level talk and high-level thinking skills (e.g., analysing, evaluating and synthesising). Teachers are central in setting up and supporting effective group-work development and support, but the particular feature of group work – perhaps its defining characteristic – is that *the balance of ownership and control of the work shifts towards the pupils themselves.*

Our notion of group work is more inclusive than any one single approach. Group work involves all children as *co-learners* and it incorporates all types of learning together – from cooperative and collaborative group work to peer tutoring and helping. Its inclusive nature is likely to encourage higher levels of participation and engagement for every child in the class.

What are the benefits of group work?

There is now a quite extensive literature on the benefits of group work in schools. In brief, it has been found to help in the following areas (see Useful references, p. 55):

- learning and conceptual development;
- school achievement;
- engagement in learning;
- oracy development;
- critical and analytical thinking skills;
- motivation and attitudes;
- behaviour in class and relations with peers.

There may also be benefits in terms of developing group-working skills and understanding of citizenship. It seems clear that we cannot teach children to behave in socially responsible and inclusive ways – this is not something that can be learned by instruction, like reading or subtraction. Behaving in a constructive way in relation to others is best furthered by children being given opportunities to discuss and recognise alternative points of view, and by being held responsible for their own behaviour in a supportive atmosphere. Children learn to get on with each other not by being taught but through everyday encounters with peers. Quite apart from these academic benefits, group work can be great fun and very rewarding. Teachers also benefit from pupil group work. When children work together in a supportive and autonomous manner, teachers are less pressed by procedural and behavioural issues in the classroom, allowing greater attention to the process of enhancing children's learning.

Why does it work?

There are several theories that explain why group work is beneficial. One view is that children's conceptual development can be facilitated by coming up against the differing views of others at about the same level of development. The 'cognitive conflict' this causes can force children to adjust and develop their own way of seeing and explaining things, and hence promote learning and conceptual development. An alternative view is that when children work together they can arrive at solutions to problems and understanding of concepts that would not have been possible if they had worked alone. Children can feed off and explore each other's ideas; they can learn together and make use of this knowledge and understanding when on their own. But in order for children to benefit from working with others, they have to want to work together as a group; they must feel safe and secure with one another; and they must feel prepared and supported in their group-working skills. Without feelings of safety and security, working in a group may result in a negative experience. This may be particularly important in the case of groups of children who might not usually mix – for example, children from different ethnic or ability groups, or girls and boys.

Why should I want to use this book?

It is not easy to develop effective group-work skills among pupils. This handbook offers recommendations for practice to help you make group work effective for you and your class. There are also ideas to help you resolve particular problems associated with group work that can arise in a class or group and suggested training activities to support pupils in developing a positive group ethos and particular group skills.

The ideas in this handbook aim to support the development of effective group work. They can be used in conjunction with and to support ideas from other educational initiatives that focus on debate and discussion, problem-solving, critical thinking and general thinking skills initiatives. These group-work practices and pupil skills may enhance the overall effectiveness of some, though not necessarily all, of these initiatives.

How to use this handbook

You are most likely reading this book as a student or teacher who is interested in group work. In our experience, the ideas presented here are best used as part of a whole-school approach to developing group-work skills in the primary school stage. If you are a teacher on your own, we feel that you will also find the content of this guide very useful; although we suggest that you may increase the likelihood of success if you work through the ideas and training activities with other teachers and colleagues.

There are a number of ways to utilise the ideas and activities presented here. We recommend that before the school year starts you read, think about and set up your classroom in preparation for group work (Chapters 3 and 4); then implement the group-training (sequential) activities to build up trust, sensitivity and respect within the class (Chapter 5). Use some of the early activities in Part II to get an idea of which children may not work well with each other (though this should not be the only reason for putting them together) before creating your groups. Try to use circle time, social/emotional education or personal/social/health education sessions to support this process and initiate the sharing of feelings and perspectives and the build up of trust. Think about how you can arrange resources and tasks in your classroom to enhance group working (Chapter 6) and how you can support group work without being too directive (Chapter 7).

At the same time, it is worthwhile to begin to use some simple forms of group work in addition to the training activities (e.g., pairs) in your lessons (Chapter 9). For example, instead of directing questions to individuals in class, ask children to find partners and have the pairs make joint responses to your questions. Ask children to share a book and take turns reading paragraphs to each other. With further training you can begin to increase the amount of group work you do with pupils across the curriculum.

We recommend that two sessions of group activities per week is the bare minimum for children to start making progress and developing group-work skills. There may be points where you would want to increase the intensity of group work. For example, during the 'storming' stage, when arguments are frequent and group work is stressful (see Chapter 4), increasing the amount of group work will help children advance. By the end of training it is important that classes periodically and regularly practise, reinforce and reflect on their group-work skills. Debriefing (see Chapter 5), or reflecting on the success (and failure) of group working, is an essential group-working skill.

You will find that you have curriculum constraints and time pressures that may prevent you from using group work as much as you would like. One successful approach is to set aside a slot for group work at least twice a week. If you persist, you will also find that there are many places in the curriculum where group and paired work can be undertaken (e.g., during personal/social/health education, literacy, numeracy, physical education, science and so on). And, as your class becomes more competent in group working, it will become easier to integrate it as part of the curriculum.

The training activities (in Part II) are as much for your benefit as for that of your pupils. These activities provide illustrations of the application of the main practices recommended in the first part of the handbook. We are sure you can improve on them both as effective activities and in terms of the fun that children have while doing them. Please be creative. And try to be supportive of colleagues who are developing and using these activities.

Developing a whole-school approach to group work

We recommend that schools and headteachers make effective group work part of the school's teaching and learning policy and that the ideas and programme expressed here are used across the whole school. This will lead to the sustained use and further development of pupils' group-work skills across the school environment. Create a special slot in your planning meetings and discuss the practices and activities (including new ones that you have found or developed). A senior member of staff should take responsibility for coordinating and ensuring that the use of group work and the development of group-work skills training are sustained. Implementing a whole-school approach requires persistence and determination on the part of the staff member responsible. Most importantly, identify the slot or parts of the curriculum where training activities can be implemented and plan your group-work activities together.

Advice from teachers.

To take on group work in this way requires a leap of faith – but it's definitely worth it!

Chapter 3

How is your classroom organised?

How is your classroom grouped for learning?

In order to make best use of the principles, practices and group-training activities in the sections that follow, it is important to think about the layout and the grouping practices you employ in your classroom.

Your classroom is a very complicated 'site' for learning and interaction. One way of developing an understanding of your classroom and the way in which you use pupil groups is to 'map' pupils and their learning activity during a lesson. Classroom mapping provides a lot of information about pupil groups and their relationship to learning. Have a look at the example below:

In this map, there are individual pupils working, a number of pairs of pupils, a small group of six pupils working with a teacher (A), and a number of subject-based tasks. Note that most of the children are working either in pairs or in a small group; some of these groups mix boys (M) and girls (F) but others are single sex. The teacher is working with only one group of pupils (Group 7). There is another adult working with an SEN boy outside of the classroom (Group 9).

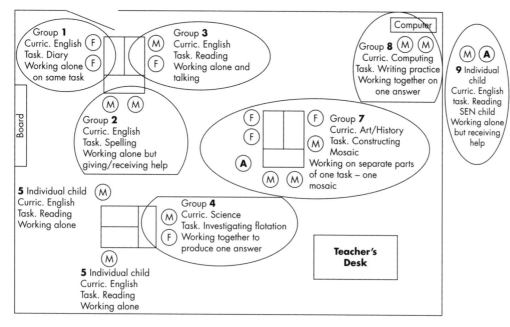

Figure 3.1 A classroom map

We suggest that you draw a map of your own classroom. Though not essential, it may be more fruitful if you do this when pupils are working together on an activity. To make a map:

1   Begin by drawing a plan of your classroom before the lesson. Include work areas, desks and other main features.

2   When a lesson is in full swing and everyone is working, bring out your plan and pencil in where everyone is seated/working (noting, where possible, boys and girls, and each child's level of attainment for that subject). Include yourself and teaching assistants in the plan. Put a circle around those children and adults who are supposed to be working together as a group on a single activity. Take a few moments to assess what is going on within each grouping or at each table.

3   During breaktime, or soon after the lesson, note down: the nature of the task in which each grouping (individual, class or group) was engaged; the nature of the interaction between pupils (working jointly on the learning task, working in parallel or working as individuals); and any other thoughts and comments relating to the extent to which children were working together, working alone, actively engaged in thoughtful conversation about the work, the extent to which they were on or passively off task or drawing other pupils off task.

When you have more time, use the mapping as a memory aid to reflect on the lesson. The following questions will help you.

* How much was the classroom activity adult led?
* How often and for how long did students get to speak?
* What proportion of the class regularly contribute to class discussions?
* Would students find value in discussing their work, views and understanding with peers?
* How much independent work was going on?
* During independent work how much talk with peers was there and to what extent was this task based or social/off task?
* To what extent did students working alone disrupt other students?
* How much group work was going on? Is there potential for more group work to be undertaken in your lessons?

The following questions relate primarily to group work situations.

The organisation of the classroom and groups

* How far were the layout of the classroom and seating arrangements conducive to comfortable group working?
* Were pupils sufficiently close together so that they could work together quietly?
* Could pupils within the groups see each other sufficiently well to allow good communication?
* Did the size of groups allow all pupils to get thoroughly involved in the group interaction?
* Were all members of the groups involved in the work and interaction or did one sex or ability level tend to opt out?

Pupils' skills and group interactions

* Did the groups work effectively?
* Was the conversation primarily focused on the work that was being undertaken?

- Were there squabbles between group members? Were children able to compromise or resolve conflicts?
- Did some pupils dominate the interaction and work?
- Did shy pupils feel sufficiently comfortable to contribute to group interactions?

Group-work task

- Did the activity encourage pupils to discuss the content of the task or were conversations mostly about resources?
- Did children in the group end up working on their own and producing their own piece of work or was there a single group outcome?

Adult role in relation to group work

- Were the children able to work independently of adult support?
- Were the children constantly seeking direction and support from adults?
- Did you encourage pupils to manage their own time?
- How far was the group work and outcome independent of an adult's input?

Think about . . .

The following may help prepare you for taking on the recommended group-work practices and group-work training activities with your class. Think about:

- When you will prepare your classroom for group work.
- How you will implement group training sessions into your weekly lesson timetable.
- How you can convince others, including your headteacher, to adopt a whole-school approach to group work.

Chapter 4

Preparing the classroom for successful group work

How should I set up the classroom and groups for group work?

Group work requires preparation of the classroom. Seating arrangements and group organisation can have a profound effect on peer support, communication and work in groups. To understand and use groups effectively in your classroom, the following will need attention:

- class seating arrangements;
- group size;
- number of groups;
- group stability;
- group composition.

Class seating arrangements

It is important that seating arrangements support group working. Flexible use of furniture and seating can make a big difference. *Using and coordinating the physical layout, seating arrangement and space to encourage pupil interaction in different working situations is the key.*

- Whole class work – best on the carpet, or facing the teacher in rows, pairs or a horseshoe. Avoid children sitting with their backs to you.
- Individual work – best done in individual seats, but if space is limited, in pairs, rows or other ways that discourage distraction, so it is better that children do not sit opposite each other.
- Paired work – best when seated in pairs/rows or as small groups where working partners sit next to/across from each other.
- Group work – best when seated in small groups around a *single* standard rectangular table or around the corner of a larger table. When children sit closer together there is less noise and they are more likely to get involved. Only increase the space if the group needs to use materials and books. Encourage children to organise themselves so that they can see each other and are not stuck out on the edge.

If the furniture is moved in set ways, and regularly, pupils become accustomed to this and movement will take less time with practice. The *physical space* available may constrain your flexibility, but even in the smallest of classrooms there are ways to adjust how pupils sit and the direction they face.

Group size

The size of groups should be appropriate to the age and experience of pupils and the purpose of the group task. Groups should normally consist of no more than four or five pupils by the end of the primary school. And the group size may be smaller when pupils are learning how to interact together and at the start of primary school. Pairs are more likely to guarantee pupil involvement than any other group size. As group size increases *free rider* behaviour (when a member lets others do all the work) becomes more probable, *communication* becomes increasingly difficult, and *diffusion of responsibility* (where no one feels responsible for doing the work) is more likely.

Pairs and threes should be used to introduce group-working to pupils.

Pros
- Simpler for pupils to work in.
- Helps build confidence for work in larger groups.
- Good for encouraging young and shy pupils to interact.
- Good when the task is complex.
- Good for peer tutoring.
- Free riding and diffusion of responsibility unlikely.
- Threes are good for practising decision-making and consensus.

Cons
- One child can dominate.
- Can be too easy if task too simple.
- In threes one child can be marginalised.

Small groups – of four to six pupils are good for many group-work activities, particularly for collaborative tasks allowing members to cope with planning, discussing, decision-making, reaching consensus, managing interruptions and conflict, staying on topic and on task.

Pros
- Good for group discussion, problem-solving, group investigations and projects.
- Good for bringing together different views.

Cons
- Small groups (four to six) represent more *risk* (threats to personal self-esteem and confidence) than smaller groups.
- Members may be less likely to speak.
- Free rider behaviour and diffusion of responsibility are more likely.

Large groups of seven to ten pupils are difficult to manage and should be used only in particular circumstances.

Pros
- Good for simple tasks involving simple interactions and gathering information.
- Good when led by an adult or very competent child.
- Work well when quickly split into sub-groupings.

Cons
- Not good for activities involving discussion, planning and decision-making tasks.
- Talk on a single topic is very difficult.
- Shy children will not get involved.
- Free rider effect and diffusion of responsibility are very likely.

LIVERPOOL JOHN MOORES UNIVERSITY
LEARNING SERVICES

Case study – group size problems

Ms Kaur wanted to use group work in her class on a collaborative task where pupils would identify and decide on the rules for group working. After briefing the class she split them into four groups of seven pupils. This resulted in:

- Some pupils doing little work, messing around and disrupting the group and class.
- Groups splitting into sub-groups: one to do the work; the other off task.
- Pupils interrupting and talking over each other.
- The topic of conversation drifting, often going off task.

The experience was very frustrating for pupils; there were many confrontations and many of the more able, conscientious pupils developed an immediate dislike for group work. Smaller groups of three–four pupils would not have led to the host of problems experienced. If pairs had been used to start the task, perhaps as a brainstorming exercise, and then fed into groups of four, which evaluated and edited the list, then the exercise would have been more productive and less frustrating.

The number of groups

Smaller groups means more groups to be monitored. In order to focus your attention on one particular group, all other groups should be able to work without your constant attention. A teacher is less likely to give full consideration and help to a particular group when multiple groups are dependent on her for low-order, procedural questions and support. If the number of groups poses a particular problem, you could think about having only a few groups working at a time while the remainder of the class works individually. However, it might be worth persisting since your teaching and management load should ease as pupils develop confidence in their group-working skills.

Group stability

Groups go through stages in their development. One well-known sequence is 'forming, storming, norming and performing'. These stages are meant to follow each other, though with new challenges groups can revert to forming and storming modes. However, the longer the group has been running, the less likely this is to happen.

Maintaining stable groups from the second week for at least the first term enables pupils to overcome insecurities and conflict by developing relationships, trust, respect and sensitivity. (We provide more information on this in the next chapter.) If groups are changed then trust building may have to be restarted. *Don't treat conflict as a reason to change the group* unless it is severe. Children need to learn how to work with others regardless of who they are. Resolving interpersonal as well as learning problems is a key outcome of effective group working.

Stages of group development

Tuckman (1965– for full reference see p. 56) identified four stages of group development:

- 'Forming' – children are unsure of each other, trust is low, insecurity and uncertainty are high, children are highly sensitive, few may contribute to the group work, one child may dominate.
- 'Storming' – conflicts and disagreements increase, cliques form, clarification of goals begins. This all indicates increased safety and is a necessary part of the trust-building process. Supportive conflict resolution strategies are needed. Personal conflict is to be avoided.
- 'Norming' – increases in satisfaction, safety, trust, tolerance of conflict, consensus and compromise, groups become more task orientated and cohesive. Conflict is managed more effectively.
- 'Performing' – increase in productivity, performance and quality, planning, problem-solving and discussion.

Case study – stable groups

Mr James had always changed the groups for different activities for a variety of reasons. He felt that stable groups were unnecessary since the class generally 'got on' and the pupils were not difficult. Furthermore, the literacy and numeracy strategies required grouping by ability, which meant that changing groups was necessary.

He decided to try stable groups for all subjects. After some initial conflicts, pupils settled into their groups and group work. They became much more proactive and worked harder. Most pupils seemed to enjoy the work and also began to support each other informally when they were not doing group work.

Group composition

Group members will not always get on with each other. If you can avoid personal conflicts, you will maximise the potential for learning. On the other hand, it is unrealistic to think that you can avoid all personal conflicts. However, incidents that lead to these conflicts can be useful in the development of group-work skills by reviewing and reflecting upon the conflicts with your children during debriefing (see next chapter).

Allowing children 'free choice' in the composition of their groups can reinforce social divisions (e.g., same gender and ability) and isolate children who are not chosen (especially those with disabilities). Children can be included in the selection of *criteria* for determining group composition. This allows pupils a say but reserves the decision for the teacher. A number of key composition criteria that can affect the effective working of groups are considered below. Fundamental to these criteria is the consideration of pupil grouping as 'inclusive' or 'exclusive'. Inclusive grouping allows children to work (and form positive relationships) with all types of children in the class – mixing ability level, gender, friendship, disability, etc. Exclusive grouping brings together children who are of similar ability, same sex, etc. This grouping practice can help to provide differentiated material/tasks for children but it may also become the basis for children to stop interacting with anyone who is seen as 'different' from themselves.

- *Ability* – This is a controversial topic. Some teaching and learning strategies recommend same-ability groups but this is for classroom management rather than for social learning purposes. Group work necessarily involves a certain amount of ability mixing. On the basis of a number of studies, it is recommended that any small grouping of children should not include the extremes (of high- and low-) ability children. *We suggest that it is best to put together high- to middle-ability pupils, and low- to middle-ability pupils.* This reduces pupil frustration due to large differences in ability while maintaining some inclusion across the ability range in your class. Able pupils benefit from working with less able pupils because they are encouraged to explain what they know/think, which helps firm up their own knowledge. Similarly, less able pupils get to know about new ideas and ways of thinking.
- *Gender mix* – An equal balance of each gender is best to encourage contact between the sexes and to prevent one gender dominating the activity. Same-gender groups may be more effective when boys or girls tend to dominate materials or the work: for example, working on a computer (usually boys) or scribing (usually girls).
- *Friendship groups* – Another controversial topic. *In practice, it may be best to balance friends with non-friends in a group.* Friends can work well as they know and (usually) trust each other, and they are better able to manage any conflict that may arise. But friendship pairs do not always work well in situations where children must help or tutor each other. Care is needed as some friends may tend to engage in off-task behaviour, particularly boys. This can be exacerbated when the class has a negative view of group work. Also, children's friendships can be 'stereotypical', as friends are often of the same sex and ability level. So if you want to promote inclusion in your classroom, you should think beyond the convenience of friendship as the basis for grouping.
- *Personality and working style* – Some pupils have conflicting personalities or may not work well together. Some children may disrupt activities, and solitary or very quiet children may hinder the group. *It is important to stop personality types dictating the success or failure of groups.* These difficulties can be used to good effect by encouraging children to speak, learn how to deal with different colleagues, and learn not to dominate. Children should be encouraged to work in groups whatever their personality type.
- *Integrating children with special needs, English as an Additional Languaeg (EAL), or isolates* may be difficult – A child may contribute little without particular support or cause conflict between group members. However, learning to work with particular individuals can greatly benefit a group. If you are trying to promote inclusion in your classroom, there is a strong argument that these children should be included in as much group work as possible. Inclusion carries a twofold value here: it helps SEN, EAL and other children to learn group-working skills that will enhance their learning and motivation in the future; and it will help other members of the class to adapt their expectations and friendship preferences to include these children. Be warned, though: this type of inclusion does not happen over night – it takes time for everyone in the class to adapt their group-working skills for inclusion. Teachers who persevere with this approach, however, report that effective inclusion of autistic and emotionally disturbed children is possible, with classmates taking responsibility for inclusion rather than relying on the teacher. Initially, careful consideration and group-work development are required in order to decide into which groups these children should be integrated.

Think about . . .

- How could you best set up the classroom to enable you to switch quickly between whole-class, individual and group work?
- Group size – some pupils may be more confident and capable of working in larger groups (of four or five). Others may be more confident beginning with partner work.
- How you will integrate particular pupils. With whom will the SEN, EAL and 'difficult' pupils work best?
- How you will react when children say they want to change groups. At what point should you let them do so?

Chapter 5

Developing pupils' group-work skills

How can I develop pupils' group-working skills?

Pupils need to be prepared for group work. Before groups can work productively, children have to be positive about working together and they must feel safe and secure in each other's company. Such feelings of safety involve pupils:

- feeling comfortable in dealing with differences and confrontations;
- believing that their ideas will be listened to and respected;
- having the confidence that they will not be embarrassed, rejected or exposed for expressing their ideas and views.

Encouraging feelings of safety and security requires what is called a 'relational approach'. This stresses the need for pupils to have the social skills to engage with each other sensitively while trusting and respecting each other. They also need to communicate effectively by listening, explaining and sharing ideas, and should be able to plan, organise and resolve problems during their group work. These skills will help them work more autonomously, be less dependent on the teacher and engage actively in learning. Group-work training activities are organised around a relational approach structured into a developmental sequence, with an emphasis on *social skills*, followed by *communication skills*, leading to more *advanced group-working skills*.

The approach that we recommend throughout this handbook emphasises the development of positive, secure and confident relationships, such as those with a parent or close friend. This approach allows pupils to develop the social skills which facilitate the development of children's responsive communication skills and allows them to engage with new problems confident in their ability to work with others. It serves as the basis for group-working skills described in this chapter (and the suggested activities in Part II) and is organised into a developmental process where more advanced skills build on earlier skills. It also promotes interaction and inclusion of children. The relational approach assumes that all children can develop their group-working skills together, initially by reorienting the classroom from focusing solely on curriculum materials to include a focus on relationships. Remember, it takes time for children to develop group-working skills. Sometimes the class may be eager to move ahead and at other times the children may need to take a step back to reinforce their trust and communication skills before they can move forward again.

Preparing pupils for group work

For group work to be effective, pupils need to understand what it involves and why they will be doing it. Some children may believe that they have little to learn from each other. Time is therefore needed to talk about how and why group work is useful and to give pupils the opportunity to contribute their thoughts and ideas. Pupils should be given the chance to develop a shared set of ground rules for their group work. They also need time, preferably after each group-work session, to debrief and reflect on what they have done, why it worked and what improvements can be made. Once children understand why they are doing group work and what is expected of them, they can begin to develop their group-working skills.

What do pupils bring to group work?

It is helpful for the teacher to try to empathise with the way in which children experience group work and how it feels for them to work with other members of their class. Many pupils may have mixed feelings about group work; some will enjoy it; others may find it frustrating and slow. Engaging in group work can be hard, especially for younger children, and emotionally wearing. Children are keen to get their own way and do not necessarily have the skills to reach a compromise or to let insignificant issues go. It is thus important to put yourself in their shoes and remember that:

- Each child brings different experiences of working with others. Whether good or bad, these experiences will influence involvement in and enjoyment of group work.
- Without group-work training, children may express a preference to work only with friends.
- Group work can leave pupils feeling insecure and unsure since they want to please the teacher and to get the work 'right'. This can discourage them from developing their own ideas and they may display reluctance to engage without adult guidance.
- The more schooling children have experienced without developing group-work skills, the more difficult it may be for them to undertake these new practices.

Part of genuinely understanding and empathising with what children experience during group work is to give them a voice, a safe and supportive group environment where they can reflect, communicate and share their experiences. The relational approach has been structured with teachers and pupils to help overcome feelings of threat and insecurity that often prevent group work from being a successful or enjoyable experience. We think that it is essential, therefore, to work with your class as it develops through the sequence of social and communication skills towards advanced group working. As your children are developing these skills, it is helpful to start small and build up group work gradually. We recommend simple activities that take place in a safe and secure environment; often it will be helpful to ask children to work in pairs. Once they have gained confidence in undertaking activities as pairs, you can begin to undertake similar activities in small groups of three to four pupils. (While the sequence and structure of the relational approach are described here, recommended activities are found in Part II.)

Social skills

Pupils need to be able to develop close, supportive relationships with everyone in the classroom – not just with preferred friends. Social skills help build up an understanding of what is involved in being a member of a group as well as the confidence to work openly with others in the group. Important social skills are:

- trust
- mutual tolerance
- mutual respect
- sensitivity to others

Leading to

- positive self-esteem
- self-confidence
- ability to deal with conflict

Activities designed to develop social skills encourage pupils to see situations from other people's perspectives. These activities are productive in building positive relationships between pupils in the group and are thus helpful in advancing group development. If the group membership changes then it is useful to go back through some of these activities to redevelop the relationships.

Communication skills

Effective communication skills have to be developed and supported. These skills help pupils communicate with each other and think about their ideas through the use of explanations and joint reasoning. As they develop, children improve in their expression of feelings, become sensitive to each other's feelings and thoughts and become more able to handle complex thoughts and ideas.

The features of group talk which are indicative of effective learning are:

- taking turns to speak;
- active listening;
- asking and answering questions;
- making and asking for suggestions;
- expressing and requesting ideas and opinions;
- brainstorming suggestions, ideas and opinions;
- giving and asking for help;
- giving and asking for explanations;
- explaining and evaluating ideas;
- arguing and counter-arguing;
- persuasive talk;
- summarising conversations.

Advanced group-working skills

Advanced group-working skills help children work together to overcome problems of difference in perspective and to organise themselves effectively so that they are less reliant on adults. This will encourage autonomous learning and responsibility for their own learning. Moreover, in many group-working situations pupils must have higher-order thinking strategies for tackling complex tasks. Some advanced group skills are:

- making group decisions and coming to consensus;
- compromising;
- encouraging all group members to become involved;
- planning the group work:
  - working out the timescale;
  - deciding whether an activity or thinking prior to group working is needed;
  - deciding whether to use roles within the group or to allocate aspects of the task to different members.

Developing pupils' group-working skills over a lesson

Pupils learn best when they are given opportunities to reflect on and then adapt their group-working skills (see figure below). This encourages children to take responsibility for their own learning and to become active in the development of their own skills. We think that each group-work training lesson should consist of three main phases within which certain activities should take place: briefing; groupwork; debriefing.

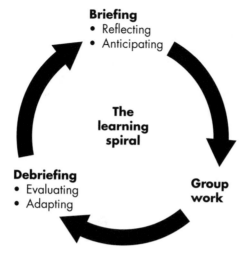

Briefing

- *Reflecting* – Discuss a particular skill such as listening, as a class or with partners/groups. Identify *what* needs to be improved or the class should reflect back to the previous group-work lesson (see Debriefing).
- *Anticipating* – Ask pupils to identify *how* they will put this improvement into practice, what they will do. This is very important because we often know what is going wrong but not what to do in order to resolve the problem.

Group work

This is where children experience group work. To help pupils focus on the skills they are to learn (identified during briefing), the teacher should remind the pupils about the behaviour they are expecting during group work. This can be written on the board under the heading 'What I'm Looking For' (WILF, described in Part II), with verbal reminders throughout the lesson.

Debriefing

Debriefing provides pupils with the valuable opportunity to reflect on what they have achieved together and how they have worked in their group. This can help the teacher evaluate how successful the session and group work were. If pupils are to present the outcome of their work, this should be done prior to the debriefing.

- *Evaluating* – Groups discuss/individuals think, 'How well did we/I do?', 'What do we/I need to change in order to improve?'
- *Adapting* – Pupils discuss evaluations and how their group work can be improved in the future. Stop children from being overly personal or critical.

Pupils should be encouraged to focus their discussion on the processes within their group: for example, feelings and emotions within the group and what, in their opinion, could be changed and improved. Here pupils have the opportunity to talk about their experience and reinforce positive impressions as well as bringing into the open any unpleasant feelings. Through reflection on their own experience and listening to each other, pupils can develop a deeper awareness about themselves, the group and the group-work process.

Briefing and debriefing are both very important as this is where reflective learning takes place. *If opportunities for reflecting and evaluating do not take place then the learning spiral is broken and children may not progress.* It is common for debriefing to be omitted because of lack of time. If this occurs, start the following lesson with a debriefing (maybe as part of the briefing). This three-phase format can be used for all of the training activities but also, from time to time, when group work is used in the curriculum (at least once per week).

Case study – practise what you preach

Ms Fernandes had been using the SPR*in*G programme of social and communication skills activities for about half a term. She noticed that her pupils were able to talk at length about how they *should* behave and interact when working as groups during the briefing part of the lesson. However, she also noticed that they would rarely behave in these ways when working as groups.

Pupils were treating the briefing, debriefing and group-work parts of the lesson as completely separate contexts and not developing their group-work skills. With effort Ms Fernandes began to bridge the gap between saying and doing by reminding pupils to focus on specific group-work skills while they were actually doing the group work. She also encouraged pupils to think about *how* they could do the skills and behave in practice and *how* they could improve the particular skill when they next did group work.

Advice from teachers.

Boundaries for group work

Be clear with the class about the 'rules' for group work. For example, during briefing and debriefing, not mentioning others' names, using the 'I' message (how it made me feel).

Think about . . .

- How you can integrate the relational skills training into the curriculum and weekly timetable.
- How you can support and facilitate the development of positive relationships within groups and your class outside of the training activities.
- How you can ensure that pupils reflect on and positively adapt their group skills in the light of their group-work experiences.
- How you can make sure that pupils 'practise what they preach' and behave in the ways they say they should.

Chapter 6

Creating effective group-work activities and tasks

How can I best organise group-work activities?

Teachers and other adults in the classroom are fundamental to the development and support of effective group working. There are a number of roles and activities that teachers and other adults can undertake to support groups.

A main way to plan for group work is by setting up each group in such a way that pupils feel safe about contributing to the group as well as planning the task so that it is challenging and legitimises group work. Developing safety within groups is part of the relational approach described in Chapter 5. Insights into how you may set up and support activities and tasks are considered here.

Creating well-organised tasks that encourage group work

Designing tasks that encourage group work is challenging. *It is important that the task is set up in a way that encourages all members to talk and work together, and does not encourage individual working.*

Case study – too many materials

Miss Hanif wanted groups of four children to work together through a number of mathematics problem-solving questions. She gave each child a sheet containing questions with spaces for the answers.

The result was a complete absence of discussion and four separate and often different answers to the questions in each group. Despite having told pupils to work together, they had worked alone. Had Miss Hanif given a single answer sheet to each group (and one question sheet), then communication between group members would have been encouraged.

A single task output

The more possible outputs there are, the more likely it is that the group will divide. It is important that groups work on a single output. One good strategy, therefore, is to give the group only a single sheet of paper on which to write or prepare their output. Groups should also be given no more than a single copy of the instructions. Of course, if the group is expected to split into sub-groups to do sub-tasks then multiple sheets of paper and pens will be needed.

Allow time for group planning

Pupils like to get on with things. In order to encourage them to plan their group work it may be necessary to withhold resources for a few minutes to allow them to organise themselves and discuss how they will do the task. Otherwise, pupils tend to jump ahead and try to get the work done before they have planned what they are going to do.

Designing different types of task

The point of group work is to get children talking and explaining ideas to each other. This means they are *actively thinking*. It is important to make sure that the task involves much more than simple activities such as cutting up pieces of paper or writing the answers to simple sums. If tasks solely focus on such low-level practical skills then the potential for group work will not be realised.

The task should be challenging for pupils, yet not too difficult. Tasks that are high in *ambiguity*, where the outcome and/or the path to that outcome are not obvious, are challenging. Ambiguity raises the need for reasoning and thinking and when conducted in a group setting leads to discussion, shared reasoning and debate to solve problems, share the thinking and make decisions. If ambiguity is too low then group members know what they have to do and how to do it, talk and high-level discussion may not be required and learning may be limited.

Tasks can also vary in terms of how *open ended* they are. Some have a single right or wrong outcome (closed), some multiple correct solutions (albeit with some solutions better than others), and some are open-ended tasks where the outcome cannot be judged as right or wrong (though they may be of better or worse quality).

Some ideas for creating open-ended tasks

- Ask questions where there are no clear right or wrong answers: for example, 'How can we make the school a nicer place to be?'
- Set an activity where the group must create something (e.g., write a piece of fiction, prepare a play, create a work of art, musical composition, etc.) given one or more criteria or constraints.
- Ask a question where there are a number of possible solutions but groups have to weigh up strategies in order to decide which solution is best or most correct.

Some ideas for creating closed tasks

These tasks have a single right or wrong outcome. A good closed task would be where groups have to think through and discuss the various strategies to reach the correct solution: for example, identify a strategy for getting across the playground without stepping on the ground; devise means for calming the traffic around the school. Discussing the different possible answers to a multi-choice question might be a poor group task.

Different types of group interaction

Group-work activities can also vary in terms of how children *work together*:

- Co-ordinating interaction – where pupils co-ordinate their actions by working on different aspects of the same task. They may take turns to do an individual gym routine, collecting and recording information, group-work roles, etc.
- Co-operative interaction – where pupils share information, experiences, views, opinions and explanations, instructing others, helping, etc.
- Collaborative interaction – where pupils work intellectually together to solve problems, make decisions, plan their work, analyse, synthesise and evaluate.

Tasks should be chosen on the basis of how demanding they are for pupils. Simple activities that require children to co-ordinate their efforts are a good introduction to group-work activities. Tasks that require children to co-operate either by sharing information or by helping and explaining ideas to other pupils are a good second step. Complex tasks may be best introduced as paired work. Once effective communication skills are developed, collaborative activities should be more frequent. Collaboration is most effective in developing and supporting high-level learning and understanding.

Structuring the group-work activity

The group-work activity can be structured so that children focus on a single goal or activity at a time. This structuring of the group work supports groups that are not yet able to plan and carry out the work as a whole. Group work can be structured:

- by splitting the task into *sub-activities*;
- through *snowballing*;
- by giving pupils different *roles* in the activity.

Sub-activities

There are multiple ways of structuring group work into sub-activities. This involves the teacher dividing the task into a number of more manageable, yet coherent, sub-activities and then guiding groups through each sub-stage of the activity.

Time deadlines for the end of each sub-stage encourage groups to knuckle down and get on with the activity (i.e., time pressure). Verbal reminders may be needed especially when the duration of the task is lengthy. However, if deadlines are too strict, they can make children feel that they are never allowed to finish anything, that the teacher does not trust them and that they do not own the work.

Splitting a task into sub-activities

- Group debate: group brainstorming (to identify the main issues) → group discussion where the issues, reasons and counter-arguments are exchanged (to apply/extend reasoning and understanding) → feedback to class.
- Solving a problem: group brainstorming (to collate possible ideas) → evaluating reasons for ideas → deciding which idea is best → applying idea.
- Group research: plan research → individuals research and learn material → share it with others → write it up as a group.
- Group experiment: make predictions and explanations → test predictions → discuss implications → prepare group report.

Snowballing

Tasks can be broken down into sub-activities and accompanied by sequencing the size of groups: for example, moving from individual work to dyads and then to groups. This is called snowballing.

Snowballing ensures everyone engages in some thinking rather than relying on others to come up with ideas. It is good for discouraging 'free riding', particularly when it begins with individual work.

Snowballing in a science experiment

1   Individuals/pairs make predictions and explanations.
2   Group (of four) shares and discusses ideas to form group predictions.
3   Test predictions as a group.
4   Discuss implications as a group.

See Chapter 9 for further ideas.

Once pupils improve at group work, you should begin to encourage them to plan the overall activity themselves (especially group research and experiments). Initially this can be conducted as a whole class where a joint decision is made about how the task will be approached and conducted. Eventually groups should be able to take responsibility for planning their work themselves. The teacher should also encourage pupils to take responsibility for keeping their work to time.

Roles

Roles can be allocated to group members to encourage a feeling of group responsibility or, for instance, to prevent the same person (usually a girl) from doing all the writing. However, *roles must be used and selected with care*. It is important that all group members are *equally* engaged in the collaborative exercise. One problem occurs when 'timekeepers' do nothing but watch the clock and do not engage in the substantive aspects of the activity, such as the generation of ideas, group reasoning and discussion. Similar problems may arise when spokesperson, group encourager and other roles are introduced. Allocating roles is probably best used when pupils are experienced at group work, but some basic roles can be introduced early on (e.g., scribe, chairperson and spokesperson). It is important that children know what the role involves in practice. Time spent discussing roles or identifying a role description is fruitful (see Part II). Teachers should initially consider identifying which child should adopt which role but once children are able to take more responsibility, allow them to decide who will take on each role.

Case study – successful task structuring

Miss Abbot wanted to use group work in her class for a collaborative decision-making task where pupils decide on the rules for group working.

After briefing the class, she encouraged the pupils to brainstorm in pairs as many rules as possible without evaluating them. After ten minutes pairs came together into fours and compared and evaluated their rules. They then selected the five most important and general rules. After fifteen minutes they fed these rules and the reasons for them back to the class and spent the remainder of the time deciding which five rules they would use as a class.

Miss Abbot found this worked very well, especially as children were able to collate some ideas in preparation for the group work. This meant that even those children who rarely contributed to group work had something to add.

Think about . . .

- How you can design tasks that encourage children to work together rather than go their own way.
- How you can structure a lesson into a set of sub-activities that help pupils do their work more autonomously.
- How you can gradually implement time deadlines so that pupils can begin to work together more efficiently and, if need be, under pressure.
- How you can ensure that pupils take on particular group roles as well as their normal responsibility to contribute to group work.

Chapter 7

The role of the teacher and other adults in supporting group work

How can I support pupils doing group work?

Adults can adopt a wide range of roles in supporting group working. However, *the notion of the teacher as the holder of knowledge which is to be transmitted to pupils is inconsistent with the benefits of group work.* Under these circumstances, pupils are prone to become passive learners and are less likely to think for themselves or take responsibility for their own learning.

In order to get the most out of group work, adults in the class need to *support and encourage* the group's attempts to do the task rather than direct the group how to complete the task.

X

Being a 'guide on the side' rather than a 'sage on the stage'

One of the main aims of group work is to encourage pupils to take responsibility for their own learning and thus be less reliant on the teacher as a source of ideas and direction. More support is likely to be needed in the early stages of the development of group-work skills. But try to decrease your intervention in group working gradually and encourage pupils to maintain the group work themselves. The adult's role is therefore to:

- *circulate* and *monitor* groups rather than work with one particular group;
- *guide* groups when they encounter difficulties;
- *model* and *reinforce* good social and conversation skills;
- *coach* individual children and groups in co-operation skills.

As your pupils become more competent in their group-working skills, you will find it easier to assume these roles. The children will become less dependent on you for direction and support, allowing you to act more effectively and reflectively in these roles.

Circulating and monitoring groups

Monitoring involves spending more time listening to what the groups are doing rather than intervening. This may be very difficult at first as many children like to be told what to do, and adults like to keep children on task. Stick with it for a few weeks, though, as children and adults will soon get used to it. However, on occasion intervention will still be necessary (e.g., to re-explain instructions, to prevent tomfoolery, to resolve conflicts or to get a group back on track).

Guiding groups

The teacher (and any other adults in the classroom) will need to support the group and intervene when necessary. This can be conducted through a *guiding* approach: working with pupils and groups in a way that encourages them to think for themselves and act responsibly. When asked explicitly for help, adults should think about making *suggestions*, giving *explanations* and asking *open-ended questions*. Try to avoid being overly directive or acting as a giver of information.

Modelling and reinforcing group-work skills

Adult intervention ought to be to the point and conducted in a way that *models* and *reinforces* good social, communication and group-working skills. Focus on talk strategies that are positive and inclusive: for example, 'What do you think?', 'Why do you think that?', 'What's your view?', 'That's a good point', 'I think this because . . .', 'Yes, but . . .' and so on. The teacher should also model and reinforce skills during briefing and debriefing.

Case study – becoming a 'guide on the side'

Miss Costa was trying to do more group work in her class. However, she was frequently frustrated by pupils' passivity: they remained very dependent on her support and assistance.

When observed by a colleague it was noticed that her interaction with groups was very directive and that she wanted the children to do the task so well that she had begun imposing her ideas on them. When this was highlighted she changed her approach by encouraging pupils to work things out for themselves and to find independent ways of getting the required information – through books and by asking other pupils for help and their views.

Initially, the pupils were resistant to this approach, which was very stressful for Miss Costa, who considered abandoning the whole project. But after some time the children settled into the new way of working, they became much more independent in their thinking and learning and they began to enjoy group work much more.

A coaching role

The teacher (and other adults in the classroom) can also take on a *coaching* role to help develop pupils' social, communication and group-working skills. This may involve advice to an individual or a group. You should evaluate current group-working skills and problems encountered and think together about how they can be developed or resolved. Again, the more that new strategies can come from the pupils, the better.

Think about . . .

- How you can model good group-work talk and interaction.
- How you can maximise and support pupil contributions during group work.
- The types of indirect intervention (guiding) that are most helpful to avoid pupils remaining dependent on your directions, questions and answers.

Chapter 8

Evaluating group work

How do I know when group work is effective?

Our experience of working with teachers and pupils has led to the identification of a number of classroom actions that indicate when group work has been successful over the year. These are some of the positive characteristics identified by teachers who have been working with us:

- Shared ownership of learning tasks and responsibility for behaviour and learning.
- Children feel safe, secure and equal with each other.
- Strong relationships built across class.
- Increased tolerance.
- Increased mutual respect.
- Positive working environment.
- Co-operative problem-solving.
- Thinking independently.
- Improved speaking, reasoning, compromise and questioning skills.
- Children supporting and helping each other.
- Children in groups able to get on with their work with minimum teacher input.
- Children and groups solving their own problems.
- Children more inclusive when socialising with peers.
- More children participating in discussions (in groups and whole class).

How can I evaluate the success of group work?

Group work needs to be evaluated so that you can take steps to resolve any ongoing problems. Problems fall into the following key areas:

- group arrangement and ethos;
- group interactions;
- role of adults;
- activities and tasks.

We have included an evaluation pro-forma at the end of this chapter that will help you and your children assess the success of group work. You should use this from time to time to review how well children are progressing in their group-work skills.

The pro-forma provides a general review of issues and ideas that we have covered in the first seven chapters of this handbook. If you are unsure about the meaning of any of the 'Aspects to look for', a quick review of the earlier chapters will help. After assessing the group work in your class, it may be useful to refer to Chapter 10 or to review your plans for preparing and supporting group work Chapters 4–7).

How can pupils evaluate their own group work?

We have also included two sheets that enable groups and individual children to evaluate their group work. Self-evaluation encourages pupils to think about how they can improve their group skills. These sheets should be used on a fairly regular basis, especially during training. The evaluations should relate to one specific piece of group work that the children have done recently. You could, on occasion, ask a child to observe groups working – however, you must ensure that feedback is constructive and used in conjunction with briefing and debriefing aspects of the Learning Spiral (see p. 23).

How can I assess group-work outcomes?

Assessing children individually can be problematic when work is carried out as a group because individual assessment can encourage competitiveness rather than co-operation. It is more constructive for group-work outcomes to be assessed at a group level or, if individual marks are still to be awarded, for them to be combined to give a group score. The latter can encourage peer helping within the group as it works to increase its score by supporting those individuals who may let down the whole group. You could ask groups to mark each other's outcomes. Some teachers have asked groups to agree on how a group mark should be divided among individuals. Great care is needed when doing this.

Advice from teachers.

Assessing group work

Two questions – 'How much have they learned?' and 'What is the outcome?' – should always be at the back of your mind.

Suggested evaluation sheets for teachers and pupils

Teacher evaluation of group work	Comments and notes
Aspects to look for: **Group arrangement and ethos** • Does the furniture arrangement allow group members to interact? • Can everyone see everyone else? • Are group members close enough to each other to hear and talk quietly? • Do children in groups lapse into smaller sub-groups (e.g., more talk in pairs than to the group)? **Group interactions** • Are all group members involved in the talk and work (i.e., no one dominates, is shy or free rides)? • Is the majority of talk on task? • Do group members show good listening skills? • Do group members take turns at talking (e.g., do not interrupt or talk over other people)? • Does group discussion involve pupils reasoning and debating together? • Do group members question each other's ideas (e.g. to clarify, to elaborate, to get reasons)? • Is the group able to reach a consensus or compromise? • Do group members give supportive and constructive feedback? • Is the group able to handle petty arguing? **Activities and tasks** • Do resources/materials encourage group work rather than individual working? • Was the task structured to support group work (e.g., snowballing, task phases, jigsaw groups (see p. 45), etc.)? • Did the task encourage pupils to discuss together/interact? **Role of adults** • Was the group dependent on an adult for completion of the task? • Did I encourage pupils to manage their time? • Did I brief and debrief pupils about working in a group? • Did I give pupils an opportunity to evaluate their own group work? • Did I remind pupils to use their group-work skills during the activity? • Did I monitor (listen without intervening) group interactions? • Did I guide pupils by asking them open-ended questions, making suggestions, etc. (rather than telling them)? • Did I model good interaction skills? • Have I given pupils opportunities to do group work in the curriculum?	

Group name: _____   **Date:** _____

Discuss each question with your group. Tick the box that shows how your group feels about how well you worked together. **Make sure you all agree on the group answer**.

Question	Yes	Some yes/ some no	No
Did everyone get involved in the group work?	☐	☐	☐
Did everyone have a chance to share their ideas?	☐	☐	☐
Did anyone encourage other people to offer ideas?	☐	☐	☐
Did everyone explain their ideas?	☐	☐	☐
Was everyone's contribution considered fairly?	☐	☐	☐
Did anyone ask questions if they did not understand?	☐	☐	☐
Was everyone happy with the final group decision/outcome?	☐	☐	☐

Write down any ways in which you think you and the rest of the group could work better together next time.

1 ....
....
....
....

2 ....
....
....
....

3 ....
....
....
....

My involvement in group work

Name: _____   **Date:** _____

What I did that helped the group	What I did that stopped the group from working well
What other people did that helped the group	**What other people did that stopped the group from working well**

How can I improve my group's work?

....

....

....

How do you think you and the rest of the group could work better together next time?

....

....

....

Chapter 9

Using group work in the curriculum

How can I start using group work in the curriculum?

The activities outlined in Part II of this book are designed to help you train your pupils in social, communication and advanced group-working skills. These training activities will be useful only if pupils also have regular opportunities to reinforce their skills and engage in group work in other parts of the curriculum. Once pupils have received some group-work skills training and become familiar with evaluating and adapting their skills, group work can be used much more regularly within different parts of the curriculum. This chapter offers suggestions for developing and implementing your own group work within the curriculum. A variety of ideas and examples are offered of different types of group work suitable for both short sessions and longer sessions that may be conducted over several lessons or even a term.

When you begin to introduce group work across the curriculum, remember to keep group sizes small (e.g., pairs), up to a maximum of five pupils for more complex activities. It is our experience that group work can be used in all curriculum areas, and every effort should be made to use it on a *regular* basis in the curriculum. This will allow pupils to get used to group work as a form of learning and provide opportunities for them to further develop their social, communication and advanced group-working skills.

Group work is most effective when it is used to *encourage supportive communication and high-level talk and reasoning*, rather than when it is used for activities like collecting, sharing and presenting information. Engaging in high-level talk may be difficult for children in KS1, but young children can still benefit from co-operation, sharing ideas and helping each other, providing a basis for more advanced forms of group work. Children may engage in more complex forms of group work if they work in pairs and the task is structured as a series of clear steps. You may be surprised at how well even young children can work as a group, as long as they have the appropriate group-working skills.

In this chapter and in the activities in Part II, we indicate the suitability of each group-work structure for different-aged pupils in the tinted heading that appears before each description. We have distinguished between LOWER PRIMARY (children aged four to seven years), UPPER PRIMARY (children aged eight to eleven years), and PRIMARY (children aged four to eleven years).

Group-work activities

Once groups are ready to engage in group work in the curriculum, some basic forms of group work can be used. Later, these simple forms of group work can be strung together to create structured but more complex forms of group work. Finally, more open-ended group projects and group debates can be used. We describe these various forms of group work with regard to their contributions and drawbacks, and provide some curriculum-specific examples. These curriculum descriptions may be extended and applied to other subjects in your class.

PRIMARY

Quick group activities

Designed to last no more than five minutes and can be conducted during a whole-class interactive session on the carpet or when seated. The most efficient way to do short-term group work is to use pairs (e.g., talk partners or think–pair–share) to brainstorm ideas/facts, to share knowledge, for one child to help another on a particular activity, or to engage in joint problem-solving.

- Pros: Encourages thoughtful involvement and equal opportunity (as opposed to whole-class interaction, where some individuals switch off). Quick and efficient to use.
- Cons: If the question/activity is not focused, this approach can lead to confusion or off-task chat. If too little time is given for a question to be explored, then learning can be inhibited and confusion reigns. An individual child can dominate.

Examples
- English: To draw out current knowledge at the start of the lesson, *brainstorm* examples of types of word or phrase – prefixes, suffixes, metaphor, simile.
- Science: To speculate, predict, explain – get children to *problem-solve* – For example, why the moon appears to change shape from a crescent to a disc.

Collecting information

Small groups are given a task where they must collect, collate and pool information. The group may divide up the task so that each member has a different job or different area to research and thus some group planning is required.

- Pros: Good for developing basic group-work planning and for giving pupils experience of how to carry out particular jobs or procedures. Good for practising research skills.
- Cons: Pupils may learn only about what they have directly worked on. High-level thinking, discussion or explanations are unlikely to occur unless there is synthesis or evaluation of the information collected (e.g., what the data means or how it relates to a theory). The best extension is to get the group to discuss, analyse and evaluate the information they have collected and then write this up.

Examples
- Mathematics: To examine the concept of probability, get groups to roll dice a number of times and to note down the sum of the numbers. They can produce a tally, graphs and so on.
- English: Group members read separate chapters of a book or separate poems and then pool their information in relation to a particular issue, summarise the chapter, and so on.

---

continued

- History: Group members may study separate sub-topics of a topic (e.g., writing, lifestyle, clothing and education of the ancient Egyptians) and then pool this information to make a group report.
- Science: Pairs or groups have different powders or sponges and pour water on to their materials. They look closely using hand lenses, monitor and record what they see happening and discuss ideas about bubbles rising. Their collective views and information are shared with other pairs or groups.

Sharing information

Pupils present knowledge/ideas/experiences about an issue or topic to the rest of the group (or class). This may require some prior (individual or group) research before it takes place (e.g., see Collecting information above and Jigsaw groups below). Best used when individuals/pairs collect information on a specific sub-topic of a group topic and then share this with the rest of the group.

- Pros: Allows groups to gain a cursory understanding of a topic or piece of information. Encourages the person doing the sharing to have a good understanding of the topic.
- Cons: Pupils may not listen unless tested afterwards. May lead to surface understanding of the main ideas but little depth in understanding or actual experience. Does not allow for high-level discussion or shared reasoning unless followed by group discussion.

Examples
- Mathematics: Talk partners – one pupil explains to another how they would go about answering a maths problem.
- Cross-curricular: School council representatives report back on a school council meeting. Pupils share experiences of their holidays.
- English: Pupils share summaries and evaluations of the books they have read recently.
- History: Pupils report back to a group on their research of a sub-topic that is relevant to the group topic, e.g. ancient Egyptian writing, hieroglyphics, education, buildings, etc.

Peer helping

Helping can be used best in mathematics, science, PE, computing and other areas that are more factually and procedurally based. The focus is on pupils telling each other about *how* to do something.

- Pros: Useful when time or equipment is limited. Allows one-to-one guidance and the pair work at the novice's pace. Can lead to good understanding of procedures in both novice and expert.
- Cons: Helping requires good understanding and ability to explain logically. The quality of help given can vary dramatically. Helpers may need training in breaking down a task into smaller steps.

Examples
- Mathematics: Pairs of children work separately on similar problems (e.g., alternate maths questions). They then come together and swap the problems they have worked on. The expert then guides the novice through the process of tackling the problem. (See also Setting problems for others to solve, p. 44.)
- Cross-curricular: The teacher explains to a group of pupils how to do a task (e.g., use a protractor or computer software). Experts develop and pool questions/problems for the novices to work on (and maybe to test them). Each expert is paired or grouped with a novice/novices and must explain to them how to do the task.
- English: More able children can support and help the less able with their reading.
- Science: Experienced children can explain to novices about how to use particular pieces of science equipment. The very advanced could explain to others about what needs to be considered and how to carry out a fair test in science.
- Physical education: Ball skills. One child supervises another while they both practise the skill, followed by how to integrate it into a series of movements and extend it.

Collaborative creation

Pupils are brought together in pairs or small groups to work together to create something new. This can be anything from writing, music or art to drama or PE. Particular criteria, themes and materials can be used to limit the open-ended nature of the creation. This form of group work may require planning on the part of pupils, especially when groups co-ordinate jobs/roles and collaborate in their activity. Pupils enjoy this form of group work as it allows them autonomy in the nature of what they do.

- Pros: Allows pupils autonomy, encourages creativity, planning, sharing ideas, explaining through high-level discussion and carrying out of the work.
- Cons: Can be time consuming. Some members might not participate; others might dominate. Children can be overambitious.

Examples
- Music: To create a piece of music using instruments (maybe that the children have made) that sounds like certain everyday activities (e.g., the path of a drop of water to the sea, a production line, a train or the tension in a story).
- English: Write a poem that uses alliteration, simile, metaphor, onomatopoeia or is in a specific form.
- Dance/science: Create a dance performance that expresses thunder and lightning.
- Art and design: Produce some artwork in a particular genre or style, or as a response to a shared experience.

LIVERPOOL
JOHN MOORES UNIVERSITY
I.M. MARSH LIBRARY
BARKHILL ROAD
LIVERPOOL L17 CBD
TEL: 0151 231 5216/5299

UPPER PRIMARY

Group debate

Pairs or small groups explore and explain differing views on a particular topic. Pupils should be encouraged to present different views, examine the reasons for them and address these views with counter-arguments and explanations. While pupils are not expected to come to a consensus or agree, they should try to persuade each other of their different views. They can, of course, agree to disagree.

Pupils do not just engage in discussions on issues that directly affect them or about which they are familiar. They can learn about, and then discuss, other issues. Under these circumstances research and an open mind are needed and the process may take much longer to collate the evidence and then to have a debate.

- Pros: Encourages depth in understanding through high-level talk and reasoning as well as analysis, evaluation and synthesis of ideas, concepts and explanations. Pushes pupils to persuade others, consider alternative ideas and change their own views.
- Cons: Can lead to heated arguments and fallings-out. May be too complex for young pupils. Can be time consuming unless good research resources (if used) are available. Some children may dominate while others take a back seat.

Examples
- Geography/PSHE: Groups debate particular issues – hot topics (e.g., fox hunting), moral dilemmas and curriculum-relevant topics (e.g., traffic-calming measures, the value of recycling, immigration, etc.)
- Cross-curricular: Structuring a debate – one pair from a group collect information in favour of a view, while another pair are against. They then listen to each other's arguments in favour and against, collect further information to counter these views and present again. Finally, the pair that looked for ideas in favour must present the arguments against the view and the other pair that collected ideas against a view must present arguments in favour. For example, groups argue the case for the benefits of being a Spartan or an Athenian in ancient Greece.
- Religious education: Learning from religion. Groups have to find out what different religions teach about vegetarianism. They have to weigh up the rights and wrongs and prepare an argument one way or the other to present in a debate.

PRIMARY

Group problem-solving and decision-making

Pairs or small groups are given a task where they must work together to solve a problem or make a decision (e.g., on a course of action). Some tasks may be closed (pupils may know what they have to achieve but not necessarily how to achieve it, and this is what they work on), while others may be much more open-ended (e.g., what to buy with school resources). Collaborative group work may benefit from a preliminary round of brainstorming or individual work that can feed into the group discussion.

- Pros: These tasks often call for higher-order thinking and reasoning and thus may be very beneficial for critical thinking and learning. The activities thus involve applying knowledge, synthesising, analysing and evaluating ideas.
- Cons: Can be time consuming, depending on the activity. Some members may dominate, be left out or free ride. Arguments may arise, making consensus difficult to achieve.

Examples
- Science: Children speculate or brainstorm individually (or in pairs) on a scientific question before discussing the question as a group. For example, which of a number of objects will float or sink, and why?
- Cross-curricular: Planning an investigation or project. Planning what information from a project to write up and present to the class. Deciding criteria on which to review other pupils' written work.
- Mathematics: Children discuss which mathematical operations to use to measure the area of the playground or the volume of an odd-shaped class-room. A more specific question might be: 'How many 2.5-litre bottles of cola will fill a 25m $\times$ 3m $\times$ 5m swimming pool?'
- Citizenship/cross-curricular: Deciding which group made a better case for a particular hot topic. For example, whether ball games should be allowed on the playground. Or which is better, being a Spartan or an Athenian (see above)?
- ICT: Prepare a presentation, web page or prospectus for the school.

Group projects/investigations

Group projects or investigations usually involve stringing together some of the basic group work structures. For example, group decision-making (planning) → collecting information → sharing and analysing information → sharing analysis with the class. Numerous combinations are possible. Projects and investigations will take time and planning, but will extend pupils' understanding of the curriculum.

- Pros: Allows pupils a lot of independence and autonomy and thus are enjoyable. Encourage planning, depth of understanding and use of lots of skills, including high-level talk, reasoning and explanation. Ideal when planning a scheme of work over a half term.
- Cons: Some members may not pull their weight. Unless adults provide a supporting role the group may get drawn in the wrong direction. Unless timing is carefully monitored by the group the task can take longer than expected.

Examples
- Science projects: Develop hypotheses, plan and carry out a test, analyse the results and write up and/or present the findings.
- Science and design and technology projects: Utilise findings from science work to identify practical ways of improving particular products: for

---

continued

> example, using a balloon to power a toy car, friction to slow down objects, micro-environments, etc.
> * English: Prepare different articles for a class newspaper.
> * History: Research houses and housing in the locality. Using different source materials, children research information about how houses and housing have changed over time. They select and organise historical information so that a corridor display can convey their findings to a wide audience.

UPPER PRIMARY

Other combinations of group work

Many combinations of group work types are possible. While there is something to be said for simplicity, a number of structures are very useful. Here are some examples.

Individual brainstorming → group-work thinking and decision-making

This is very useful as it encourages all children to engage in some preparation and thinking prior to engaging in a discussion, ensuring that everyone does a bit of work and has something to contribute.

> **Examples**
> * Science: Encourage pupils to make predictions and explain their reasons about what will or will not happen: for example, what will and will not grow and why.
> * English: Brainstorm persuasive words to use in a flyer to drum up support for an issue or to act on an issue (e.g., lobbying the headteacher to extend lunchtime play).
> * Religious education: Explore the meanings behind signs and symbols of a range of religions. Class brainstorms ideas about signs and symbols they know, sharing information. Groups collect information about the signs and symbols of different world faiths. They note associations with times of the year when these signs and symbols are incorporated into rituals. Groups use this information to design a symbol to convey something that children commonly identify with and feel plays a significant role in their lives.

Setting problems for others to solve

Brainstorming → decision-making → problem-solving → peer-helping

This combination uses a variety of different types of group working strung together to give a powerful learning situation which is particularly useful in maths. It is also useful to do stages 1–3 alone.

1   Devise problems in pairs

2   Pass problems to next pair along line

3   Pass problems back to original pair for marking.

4   One member from the pair explains to one member from the other pair where that pair went wrong.

5   Pairs reform and one child explains to the other where they went wrong.

Jigsaw groups

Collect information → share information → peer-helping/ share information →group report

1   Used where the class studies a main topic (e.g., pollution, recycling) in which there are a number of sub-topics (e.g., car pollution, power stations).
2   Groups of four each research a specific sub-topic. The group may have a large pile of books and each person can skim through a couple to get as much information as possible on the sub-topic and then feed it into the group. The group becomes *expert* on the specific sub-topic.
3   The group is then split up and each expert member becomes a member of a new group consisting of experts who have studied different sub-topics. Each child *shares (teaches)* what they have learned with the rest of the group. The group (or individuals) write a booklet/report on the overall topic.
4   This can be followed by an assessment on the overall topic, and group scores are given based on the sum of individual scores or lowest individual score. This encourages experts to make an effort to explain (teach) what they have learned to their group, and equally the group will make an effort to learn.

Examples
*   Science: Different types of bones, species of insects, animal life-cycles, etc.
    – more reference-based work is good for this type of group work.

---

continued

- Geography: Pollution, global warming, recycling, etc.
- Art: The life and works of a specific artist and their different styles of artwork, methods, etc.
- History: Fashion, money, society, justice, education, etc. in a certain historical era or civilisation.

Other useful combinations

Brainstorming (group) → evaluating reasons for ideas (group debate) → deciding which idea is best (group decision-making)

This may be used to plan a group project, or what to do in a collaborative creation or as part of a problem-solving exercise.

Learn/research material (individuals/pairs) → share it with others (groups) → write it up/test each other (groups)

This format could be used in research sub-topics of a group topic (e.g., humanities subjects). Groups learn the material that individual members have collected and then are tested and write everything up as a group or even in individual reports.

Plan investigation (group decision-making) → collect data (group collection of information) → analyse data (group debate) → discuss implications (group decision-making)

This format would be typically used when conducting a science investigation from start to finish.

Predict and explain (individual thinking) → discuss predictions and explanations (group decision-making) → test predictions (groups collect data) → discuss results (group decision-making)

Also could be used in science to formulate hypotheses and discuss understanding of the science concept under study.

Chapter 10

Troubleshooting

Resolving common group-work problems

Introduction

Working with teachers over a number of years, we have encountered and overcome a number of problems concerning group work. Below, we provide examples of problems and offer ways to overcome them. In addition to the specific recommendations, we remind readers that many group-working problems may arise from lack of trust and support among group members. As we recommended in Chapter 5, the relational approach (developing social, communication and advanced group-working skills) underlies effective group work. When children encounter problems working with one another, it may be useful to draw upon/return to fundamental trust and communication activities to reinforce group solidarity and stability.

Group members do not practise what they preach

Children are often very good at telling you how they should act during group work but often do not behave in this way. This is an important issue to overcome since it is the *doing* of the group-work skills that we are trying to change.

We can get around this problem by emphasising the main skills that are to be learned and practised throughout the lesson but particularly when *briefing* the practical activity. Most important is following up and discussing how pupils can develop their skills during the *debriefing*.

During the briefing part of the lesson and immediately prior to the group-work activity:

- Emphasise to pupils that the practical activity is a chance to *practise* the particular skills.
- Spend time talking with pupils not just about what they should be doing but about *how* they can do it in practice.
- Get pupils to *anticipate* what problems may arise and how they should deal with them when they arise: for example, how they will deal with conflict.
- Emphasise to pupils *behaviour that you are looking for* during the group work (write this on the board), remind them during the group work and then follow this up at the end.
- *Model the behaviour* either directly or by participating in the activity with a pupil.
- *Reinforce* and highlight some of the group-work skills when using group or paired work in the curriculum.

During the group-work activity:

- Stop pupils during the activity to remind them of the objective or the skill they should be practising/thinking about ('What I'm looking for' – WILF – is described in Part II, p. 59).

During the debriefing part of the lesson, encourage pupils to:

- *Reflect* on their behaviour and group interaction so that they can do it better in the future.
- *Evaluate* how well they performed the particular skill/s.

Following these guidelines will help to raise pupils' awareness of the skills they are supposed to be practising, but more importantly it will give them ideas and ways in which they can put their skills into practice and indicate how they can adapt and develop those skills.

Some group members do not get involved in the group work

All group members are supposed to contribute to the group, but there may be a number of reasons why pupils do not get involved in the group work. They may be free riding, they may be shy, they may have personal reasons for not engaging with others, or they may be discouraged from involvement.

Free riders: leaving the work to others

We can get around this problem by:

- Making greater use of small groups (up to four) and paired work unless the groups can be broken down into sub-groups to do different aspects of a task (e.g., see structuring the group-work activity, p. 27).
- Using 'snowballing' – where individual or paired work feeds into small group work, formed by combining pairs. Using individual work to feed into larger groupings can ensure that everyone has done at least some work in preparation for the group work.
- Allocating roles to group members each time a piece of group work is started so that particular children are not always able to opt for the easiest role (e.g., timekeeper) and are given opportunities to develop their group-work skills.
- Making individuals accountable to the group. You could evaluate individuals on their contributions to the group work. Alternatively, you could base the group assessment on the sum of individual assessments (or the lowest-scoring member provides the score for the whole group) or group members' contribution to the group work. You could also structure the task so that group members are interdependent by allowing only particular members access to essential information or knowledge required by the group to complete their task.

Shy children

- Shy children may find it easier to contribute in pairs, and more so with friends. Try to make sure that if they are in a small group they are with at least one friend. Build up groups with shy children much more carefully from pairs to threes and then fours.
- Stable groups breed familiarity between pupils in terms of procedures, trust and positive conflict and are thus good for encouraging shy pupils.
- Encourage shy children to participate and give them positive feedback. Part of the reason for their shyness may be a lack of confidence.
- Do not discourage them by pushing them into high-risk roles (e.g., spokesperson) too early.
- If shy children are attentive and understand the work well it may be better to allow

them to participate by just listening to the group discussion. As long as they are actively involved when work needs to be done then the rest of the group should not become frustrated with them.

- If, after repeated attempts, shy children remain unforthcoming, group them with other shy children or encourage them to take a bit of a risk with a chairing or spokesperson role.

Ignoring or excluding non-participants

Sometimes it is easier to ignore those who do not contribute to the group work. However, this does not resolve the problem and may even reinforce it. Not listening to others' contributions, interrupting and talking over others can all have a debilitating effect on the group ethos.

- Sometimes pupils have natural difficulties speaking to more than one or two others and often talk simultaneously, interrupt or ignore others. Using smaller groupings can overcome this.
- Remind the group of how important it is for all of them to participate and encourage them to elicit contributions actively from those who do not participate.
- Assess the group or get the group members to evaluate themselves on their level of participation and listening. Alternatively, the teacher or a pupil observer could assess the group. When this becomes part of the group evaluation or outcome non-participants are more likely to be encouraged to join in.
- Group roles can be allocated by the teacher so that weaker pupils remain involved or dominant pupils do not take over.
- Have a quiet word with non-participants and encourage them to join in. Find out if there is a good reason for them not joining in. It may be that others have not appreciated their contributions in the past or that they have been ignored.
- Non-participation may be an indication that the group member is struggling with the task (they may disagree with it or feel it is irrelevant to them).

To encourage listening to others:

- During briefing or debriefing ask group members how we show we are listening and what it feels like when they are not listened to or are interrupted. Ask them to think about how they can help someone who does not listen to them.
- Introduce a task where group members note down the gist of what others have said. In the debriefing you could suggest that those who did not feel they did this very well could try harder to listen to others in future.
- Emphasise during briefing and the lesson that you are looking for evidence of listening to and involvement of others. This could be written on the board as 'What I am looking for'. You could pick up on those who are not listening. You could also explicitly evaluate group members on their listening and inclusive behaviour.

Groups split into smaller groupings

Groups may split into smaller groups for any number of reasons. This can be due to the use of large groups, materials that encourage individual working and pupils not being sufficiently close together.

- In large groups pupils who are inexperienced in group work may have problems speaking and listening to all of the other children in the group. Smaller groupings can overcome this. Think about reinforcing social and communication skills in these groups.

- Multiple pens and sheets of paper to write on or to read from often lead to a group splitting into smaller sub-groups/individuals or arguments about what colour pens to use and so on. The better tasks have tended to involve groups or pairs working with just one large piece of paper and a single pen.
- Too much space or obstacles between group members encourages groups to break into sub-groups or members to be edged out of the group. A group of four around a single rectangular table encourages pupils to work as a whole group. If more space is needed later for the practical activity then a second table (but no more) can be added. If the groups need more space then sitting on the floor can allow proximity and the space to do the work. Furniture removal takes up time and is demanding on the teacher. With consistency and practice, the time taken to do this can be reduced.
- Pupils should be encouraged to think about where they will sit in relation to each other so that they can see, speak, listen and interact with the rest of the group easily. Encourage face-to-face seating with at most two in a line.

The group is unable to handle conflict, make decisions or reach a compromise or consensus

Pupils often find it difficult to make joint decisions or to resolve conflict. Conflict is quite normal in group work and actually is a main impetus in the success of group working. It is also a central stage in a group's development – unless particular issues are resolved the group is unable to perform to the best of its ability. It is important, however, to avoid petty disputes that are unresolvable.

Conflict about ideas that are central to the task can be advantageous as long as members are encouraged to explore each other's reasoning with a view to coming to a compromise or consensus. Sometimes people have to agree to disagree and the teacher should explain that it is not a bad thing to hold different views. However, this should not be used as an excuse to prevent group members from debating the issue in the first place. You and your pupils should not allow conflict to destroy the group.

- Conflict is a major difficulty that children face and thus they may benefit from class discussion of specific instances to resolve or learn from them.
- Clear ways of dealing with conflict may need to be agreed upon and incorporated into the ground rules for group working.
- Get pupils to anticipate what problems may arise and how they will deal with them when they arise: for example, how to deal with conflict, what to do to come to a consensus and so on.
- Encourage pupils to think about how a compromise could be reached.
- Make it part of the chair's role to mediate, have the last word, suggest a compromise and so on.
- Establish ownership of the conflict. Which members of the group feel the conflict and are being affected by it? Include those members of the group who are not directly involved in the conflict. How does the conflict make them feel? Also distinguish between people, actions and opinions so that actions that cause conflict are resolved and differences of opinion are discussed.
- It might be useful for children to write down their thoughts about the conflict. This gives them time to think through the conflict when alone and away from an emotionally charged situation.
- Allow pupils an opportunity to have time out so that they can escape from the conflict. Allowing this means that they do not feel trapped and are more likely to try to resolve the conflict. As a last resort, allow them to change groups. However,

individual pupils should not be allowed to do this too often as they will gain a reputation as a troublemaker.
- Consider repeating some trust and communication activities with the group/class.

Group members disrupt the group or class

This can be a tough nut to crack. Though it takes less courage to be disruptive in small group situations than in class settings, teachers should not consider resorting to whole-class instruction. Disruption in a group is often restricted to a very small proportion of the class, thus allowing the remainder to get on undisrupted. On some occasions there may be no easy solution other than restructuring the groups.

- First make sure that it really is disruption. It might simply be a healthy, if heated, group discussion.
- It may be useful to ask yourself whether the disruption is aimed at others within the group, others in another group or even at the teacher. Quite often, disruptive behaviour can be for the teacher's benefit.
- The disruptive behaviour may be a symptom of a dysfunctional group: for example, if one sex is dominating the group task (girls are as culpable as boys), group members mistrust each other and so on. It is thus important to find out why group members are being disruptive.
- Try to encourage the disruptive child's contribution to the group by focusing on their positive contributions.
- You could have a chat with the disruptive child and see if they have any reasons for being disruptive. Ask them what would help them not to be so disruptive.
- Ensure that tasks have clear and definable goals.
- Friendship groups may result in disruption if the class does not have a positive view of group work.

Group members do not do their jobs

This can be a particular problem, especially when pupils are given roles that come into play only for a short period of the task: for example, spokesperson or timekeeper.

- Structuring the task with short deadlines may keep group members on their toes. Remind the group that their deadline is approaching or that they should be starting a particular aspect of the task.
- It may be useful to have the task instructions written on the board or on sheets of paper to ensure that pupils know what they are to do.
- You could also try to ensure that the first part of the task is short and simple so that all are engaged from the start. If the group has to start by making complex decisions from the word go, this can be a licence for some to let others get on with it.

Solutions specific to group-work roles

Some pupils get caught between performing their role and being a group member, resulting in acting out just one role or doing a bad job of both. Other children are unsure how to perform their role in practice.

- Ensure that group members know what is involved in their roles and how the role can be put into practice. This is better written down, maybe as a job description. Emphasise that roles are in addition to being an active group member. This could be a feature of group rules.

- Allocate roles to pupils rather than allowing them to choose their own (at least at first) so that the complexity of the role is matched to the ability of the child.
- Encourage pupils to see their role as a group member as more important than their specialised role.
- Only use roles when really necessary.

Group work starts off well but then fades

This can happen when too much time is allowed for group work, when groups have had a break or when the main aim of the activity has been completed.

- Keep the group busy. Consider giving short deadlines and or giving the group too much work to complete in a given time period (although you will have to allow time for finishing at a later point). Use this strategy with care, since pupils get annoyed when they are not given enough time to complete their work.
- Make the final stage of group work important for learners. This can be where they are assessed, or where they think about the lessons they have learned from group work.
- Get the group to summarise what they have done at the end and make this an integral part of the task: for example, to feedback to the rest of the class.

A member dominates the group or is over-talkative

Dominant characters can be a particular problem, especially when they want to do everything. They may be well intentioned but they need to be discouraged from dominating the group. This can be handled in a number of ways:

- Have a class discussion on the pros and cons of dominant group members. Get pupils to reflect on how dominant they are and to talk about when they feel they have been too dominant or not sufficiently dominant.
- Have a quiet word with the dominant pupil. Emphasise your pleasure that they are so keen to contribute but encourage them to let others contribute too and take more of a lead role. Suggest that they say only some of the things that they think so that they avoid trying to fill every silence. They could also encourage others to speak up.
- Allocate roles to the group and give the dominant member a less centrally involved role or maybe even encourage them to observe the group or another group containing a dominant child.
- Have a discussion with the group encouraging them to reflect on how they are functioning. Ask them various questions about how well the group is working and then slip in questions about who said the most, whether someone spoke too much, whether someone took the lead, whether there was anything they thought but did not say, why they did not say this, and so on.
- Remove the person from the group and put them in a group where members are more assertive in speaking up.

Some members act like know-it-alls

The group ethos and ability to get the work done can be restricted by know-alls. Some of the suggestions for dominant group members can be applied to this problem. Also:

- You could allow the group to sort out the know-all themselves. The group will be keen to tell the know-all when they are proved wrong. It may be prudent to step in at this point and have a word with the person showing the know-all behaviour. If you do not intervene, the group ethos may deteriorate.

The group is very passive

Sometimes groups can be very passive and avoid making decisions or having discussions. They are often extremely dependent on the teacher. This usually occurs when group work is first introduced. Pupils will feel insecure and unsure what they are to do, and may be concerned about getting the 'right' answer.

- You need to allay their fears. Avoid being too directive or critical. Tell them that there are no right or wrong answers (though some answers may be better than others).
- Encourage groups to find out things for themselves. Where could they look to find the piece of information they need?
- Allow groups to discover things for themselves and to learn from their mistakes.
- Avoid changing the group's ideas – pupils can feel very dejected when an adult changes their ideas or actively rejects them. At most, suggest a variety of ideas.
- If the group is uncritical of ideas (i.e., they accept ideas without discussion), the teacher could try to introduce some conflict by questioning whether anyone disagrees with the view or can challenge the consensus.

The group does not engage in discussion

Pupils often do not engage in much discussion but rather get on with the practical activity of writing. This may be because they feel a pressure to produce the work or to appear as though they are getting on and achieving something.

- Explicitly set time aside for group discussion before starting the practical work.
- Withhold materials for the practical side of the task until the groups have finished their discussion or for a set amount of time.
- Avoid the practical side of the task altogether if it really is unnecessary.
- Structure the discussion with some specific questions to make it clear what you want the pupils to discuss and how to go about doing it.
- It may be helpful to review the role of exploratory talk in your class. Neil Mercer's Talk programme (Dawes et al., 2000 in Useful references on p. 55) may be helpful.

The group spends too much time talking off task

Group-work situations are most beneficial when the talk is on task and members learn from each other by explaining things to one another. One of the major benefits of group learning is its informal nature, as long as social chatter does not prevent the group from achieving its aims. There are various ways to deal with off-task talk:

- Check that social chat really is a problem. You may find that it is infrequent and sometimes it forms part of an explanation between group members.
- Your proximity to the group should reduce the amount of social chat, so make more frequent visits to the vicinity of the group.
- If off-task chatter becomes a serious problem and is not just restricted to isolated occasions, you could consider discussing this with the group and bringing up the problem in debriefing.

Some group members criticise others

A negative group ethos is a significant contributory factor in the failure of group work. Putting others down for their ideas or inability to do particular tasks is a main cause of a negative group ethos. When pupils are so used to having to compete with other children in the class for rewards and praise, it may be difficult to break out of a cycle of derogatory comments between them. There also can be a fine line between positive, constructive feedback and regular negative (though maybe similarly constructive) feedback.

- Discourage pupils from dismissing the ideas of other group members. Encourage pupils to find something positive to say about each other's ideas.
- Have a discussion about maintaining a positive group atmosphere where pupils think about how they felt when others put them or their ideas down. Raise the issues of anger, frustration, revenge, low self-confidence and similar feelings and ask what effects they may have on group working.
- Encourage children to watch their language (avoid negative language like 'poor', 'bad', 'unsatisfactory') and body language (sighs, grimaces) which may cause problems by hurting other people's feelings.
- Step back and repeat some trust and communication activities.

Gender issues are disrupting the group

Gender issues can arise during group work. The easiest way to avoid these problems is to take the necessary steps in the first place (see Group composition, p. 17):

- Balance the sexes within a group. If this is impossible then ensure that where a child of one sex is in a minority that they either get on with the other children in the group or are sufficiently strong in character to stand up for themselves and not feel isolated.
- One sex may often talk off task while the other does the work. If possible, have two boys and two girls on a rectangular desk, with each girl facing a boy across the desk.
- Try to prevent boys from taking charge of the equipment (computers, science or sport apparatus).
- Avoid encouraging competition between the sexes or siding with one or the other (if this ever happens).

Group work is disorganised

If groups are poor at organising their group work then they will not be able to achieve the task very well. This is particularly a problem in creative tasks, when pupils are keen to get on with the doing of the activity.

- Scaffold the groups' planning and organising of the task. Initially you may wish to structure the task yourself and set short deadlines, regular reports back to the class, and repeated reminders of the timing of the activity (i.e., what they should be starting or finishing at that point). Ask pupils to think together about how they will approach the task during the briefing phase of the lesson. Encourage them to devise a plan of action.
- Once pupils are better at thinking about how they will do the task, allocate time at the start of the group work where pupils are expected to plan what they will do and how they will do it.

Pupils' group-work skills are not improving

There may be a number of reasons why pupils' group-work skills do not improve. Think about whether the problem is that they are not applying and practising what they see as good group-work skills or whether they are just not building on their skills.

- Look at the suggestions in Group members do not practise what they preach, above (p. 47).
- Ask pupils how their specific skills are developing. Get them to self-evaluate after group work and encourage them to think about how they can improve their skills in the future. Remind them of this immediately prior to future group work.
- Repeat earlier trust and communication activities.

Motivating pupils

Some children just will not do group work. These children may be uncompromising and disruptive in the group, or may try to free ride or attempt to work independently. They need to learn that group work can be fun and that they have more to gain from doing it. This might mean creating extrinsic rewards (e.g., merits, stars, competition rewards, marbles/tokens) to draw them in, in the hope that intrinsic rewards will then take over.

- Give greater value to the group product and encourage taking part in group work, for example by giving the whole group an extrinsic reward when the child is involved and has worked well with others.
- Introduce some sense of competition or evaluation of the products. Each of the other groups or individuals could award points (discreetly) under different criteria for each group output (never their own). Then the points could be added up to find a winner, but not a loser.
- Allow the child to opt out, but encourage them to take on an observer role so that they can look for good group work, communication and so on.
- Move the awkward child to a successful group that is stable and mature enough to cope with them and value their contributions, especially when they compromise, etc. This is risky, but after a few attempts things may settle.
- Encourage the child to take a risk – by compromising, or being quiet, or not being argumentative or fussy.

Useful references

Cowie, H. and Rudduck, J. (1988) *Learning Together: Working Together*. London: BP Educational Services.

Curry, M. and Bromfield, C. (1998) *Circle Time In-service Training Manual*. Tamworth: NASEN.

Dawes, L., Mercer, N. and Wegerif, R. (2000) *Thinking Together: A Programme of Lessons and Activities*. Birmingham: Questions Publishing.

Dunne, E. and Bennett, N. (1990) *Talking and Learning in Groups*. London and Basingstoke: Macmillan Education.

Farivar, S. and Webb, N. (1991) *Helping Behavior Activities Handbook: Cooperative Small Group Problem Solving in Middle School Mathematics*. Los Angeles: UCLA.

Fountain, S. (1990) *Learning Together: Global Education*. Cheltenham: Stanley Thornes.

Gillies, R.M. (2007) *Cooperative Learning: Integrating Theory and Practice*. London: Sage.

Hall, E., Hall, C. and Leech, A. (1990) *Scripted Fantasy in the Classroom*. London: Routledge.

Kutnick, P. and Rogers, C. (1994) *Groups in Schools*. London: Cassell.

Leech, N. and Wooster, A.D. (1986) *Personal and Social Skills: A Practical Approach for the Classroom*. Exeter: Religious and Moral Education Press.

Mercer, N. (2000) *Words and Minds: How We Use Language to Think Together*. London: Routledge.

Race, P. (2000) *500 Tips on Group Learning*. London: Kogan Page.

Stanford, G. (1990) *Developing Effective Classroom Groups*. Bristol: Acora Books.

Thacker, J., Stoate, P. and Feest, G. (1992) *Using Group Work in the Primary Classroom*. Crediton: Southgate Publishers.

Tuckman, B. (1965) Developmental sequence in small groups. *Psychological Bulletin*, 63, 384–99.

Part II

Group-work and training activities for your class

Introduction

Children's progress at school will be affected by the quality of relationships in class and their positive attitude. These can be aided by teachers ensuring that experiences help children develop a positive sense of themselves and constructive relationships with others. This section outlines a relational approach based on a number of social, communication and advanced group-work skills activities. The activities have been ordered into a developmental progression of complexity, with certain activities building on others (as explained in Chapter 5). We suggest that your class undertakes two or three activities per week at the start of the school year, progressing from initial social skills (trust, sensitivity) through communication and advanced group-working skills that can (eventually) be integrated into curriculum-based tasks. Remember that the activities are progressive; and it is often worthwhile repeating some of the earlier activities when/if your pupils' group working becomes tentative or ineffective. Also, note that this is an indicative listing. You can develop the activities by adjusting the content or duration, or by extending the ideas and group work into other areas of the curriculum. You can also develop and use your own activities and may find many other sources for further group working.

Age suitability

As described in Chapter 9, we have divided age-appropriate activities into LOWER PRIMARY, UPPER PRIMARY and PRIMARY to cover age groups four to seven years, eight to eleven years and four to eleven years, respectively. You will notice a heading at the start of each section indicating the recommended age range for the activity. However, this age range is only a rough estimate to give you a quick guide: you will find that some younger children are capable of undertaking an 'older' activity, and older children may enjoy a 'younger' activity.

Stable groups

You will notice that many of the tasks refer to the use of stable groups (see Chapter 4). You should use these activities to help determine the groups that you plan to use. It is quite important that children do the activities in the groups that they will be in for a substantial period of time. The activities are about building up relationships, trust, respect and so on between group members to help them work better together; this will not happen if the groups are frequently changed.

WILF – 'What I'm looking for'

One difficulty that you may encounter when working through the activities is that pupils are very good at saying what they should do but are poor at putting it into practice. The trick is to connect the group-work activity explicitly to the briefing discussion beforehand, since these activities are 'opportunities' for pupils to try out their skills. Teachers can also encourage the practical use of communication skills by ensuring pupils use ground rules for group talk and by emphasising the skills that the teacher is looking for (we use the heading 'What I'm looking for' – WILF). In this way you can note (on the board or elsewhere) what skills and behaviour you would like to see when pupils are interacting, and you can remind them of these during the group-work activities.

Safety and security of your pupils

As we have stressed throughout this handbook, children need to develop their group-working skills from a basis of trust, security and sensitivity. It is important that the classroom environment (or wherever your class undertakes these activities) also provides a place of safety and security. Each activity asks children to become involved either physically or psychologically. For children to engage fully in these activities, it is best to arrange the environment so that there is:

- little likelihood that a child will stumble over an obstacle;
- enough room for all children to move around without bumping into each other;
- enough equipment for all children to participate at the same time (or in a particular order).

You must check your school's health and safety policy for guidelines. As the teacher, you should consider how well the children are briefed, so that they understand and are able to undertake the activity. You should also keep a sharp lookout for any potential conflict (as discussed in Chapter 10) and any possibility of an accident taking place. Once your class begins to develop and become more confident in their group-working skills, many of these safety and security issues will be resolved as second nature. And, as you and your class become more competent in using the skills, everyone will enjoy engaging in these activities. *If you are in any doubt about the suitability of a session or activity for your pupils, do not use it.*

Below, we suggest a range of activity sessions, but first there are some important points to note:

- Sessions can be used flexibly – from thirty minutes to over an hour in length.
- Timings are approximate and can be extended or reduced as appropriate.
- The activity sequence is developmental and thus group-work activities should not be used selectively or in different sections (although you can always draw upon/repeat previous activities).
- In most cases the expectation is that the groups used are the *stable groups* you set up towards the start of the term.
- It is essential that you allow time for *briefing* and *debriefing*, as these are the times when pupils are thinking and learning about how to develop their skills.
- The *teacher information sheets* are designed to help you carry out the lesson and group activities.
- There are also *worksheets* for pupils which you can photocopy.

Group work and group-work rules

Resources

1 pen and paper per group

Learning objectives

- To think about working with others.
- To develop rules for working with others in pairs and groups.

Briefing (15–20 minutes)

Hold a class discussion about working with others in pairs and groups. This is your chance to find out what children think about working together and what their expectations are.

Explain to pupils that this year they will be working together a lot, maybe more than they have before. Find out what they think about working together.

- Do they enjoy it?
- Do they think they work better when working with others?
- Do they think they learn more?
- Do they prefer working with a partner or in groups?
- What sorts of people (discourage identification of others by name) do they think they work with best: friends, more able, less able, same ability, girls, boys, etc.?
- How can they expand their work choices?

Explain that in order for groups and pairs to work well together, they will need to decide on some ground rules for their group work.

Group work (10–15 minutes)

Ask groups (of two to four) to brainstorm ten rules for group working. They should note these on a large piece of rough paper. Give them five minutes for this. They then should spend the next five to ten minutes choosing what they believe to be the four most important rules.

Class work (10–15 minutes)

Have each group report the four important rules they chose and write them on the board to form a class list. As a whole class, try to reduce the list down to five main rules. The resulting rules should be incorporated as guides for class behaviour and displayed around the classroom. Good examples of rules might draw on the following:

- Involve everybody and encourage others to speak up.
- Trust and cooperate with each other.
- Respect each other's views and ideas.
- Take turns to speak, don't interrupt.
- Listen actively.
- Help and support each other.
- Suggest and share ideas and information.
- Support ideas with reasons.
- Think of alternative ideas and reasons.
- Be prepared to change your view.
- Take responsibility for your group and the work.
- Be positive about working together.

Debriefing (10 minutes)

Ask groups how they got on in their group work. What was positive about working together? What did not go so well? What would they try to improve next time and how will they go about doing that?

Follow-up work

Try reviewing the rules for working together later in the term as ideas will move on once the children have had a chance to get used to group work.

Sensitivity and awareness

PRIMARY

Below are five activities for developing sensitivity and awareness of others. These can be used separately with briefing and debriefing to form a thirty-minute session or in combination to form longer sessions.

Resources

Tasks 2.1–2.4 require space such as that in a gym or hall. Task 2.2 requires pieces of string or chalked lines long enough for at least eight people to stand on. Task 2.3 requires one or more large gym mats or something similar to act as a turtle shell.

Learning objectives

* To develop an understanding of trust, openness and sensitivity to others.
* To have fun with other members of their group and class.

Task 2.1 – Mirror, mirror

Time: Two to three minutes for each pairing. Rotate children so that each child has worked with three or four different partners from their group by the end.

Group size: Create pairs from stable groups.

Briefing: How can you make sure you co-operate with each other in this task? It is best to begin with something simple and then progress to more difficult actions. Try not to explain what you are doing – just act it out and wait for your partner to mirror it.

Task: Pairs of children stand facing each other, approximately half a metre apart. One child should be designated as the actor; the other is supposed to be their mirror image. Give the children some 'scripts' to follow (see below), where they act out everyday activities. Tell the actor that they can do or say anything but that their partner can only follow their actions (since mirrors do not speak, etc.). The roles can then be reversed, with another 'script'. Possible scripts:

* Waking and getting up in the morning
* Getting ready for school
* Sitting and working in class
* Playing basketball/netball in slow motion

Debriefing: What did you find easy/difficult? Did you get better at copying as you worked together or was it more difficult as the expressions and actions became increasingly complicated? Were the actions harder to copy with a new partner? How well did you co-operate with each other?

Task 2.2 – Crossing the river

Time: Minimum of ten minutes for groups of eight; longer if a larger group.

Group size: Begin with groups of eight (combine stable groups) and extend gradually to the whole class.

Briefing: The whole group must work together to solve the problem. What are you going to have to think and plan before making your first move? What will aid co-operation?

Task: A piece of string or a line drawn with chalk is made to represent a bridge. Pupils are asked to line up along it. The teacher tells the group that the bridge spans a river full of crocodiles and piranha. The group task is to line up alphabetically, without letting anyone fall into the river. They must always have at least one foot on the bridge. Maybe put an 'obstacle' on the bridge so that swapping places becomes more difficult.

Debriefing: How did you help each other to line up? At what point in the task was co-operation most difficult? At what point in the task did co-operation become easier? What have you learned from this exercise?

Task 2.3 – Big turtle

Time: Ten minutes.

Group size: Begin with stable groups (fours) and gradually extend by adding members from another stable group.

Briefing: As for Task 2.2.

Task: A group of between four and eight pupils (wearing suitable clothes) get on their hands and knees under a large 'turtle shell' and try to move across the room. A gym mat works well as a shell but other materials – such as cardboard, a sheet, etc. – may be used. You could set up a course for the turtle to try to manoeuvre around without losing its shell.

Debriefing: As for Task 2.2.

Task 2.4 – Group breathing

Time: Ten minutes.

Group size: Start with pairs (from stable groups) and then gradually increase in size to involve the whole class in one big circle, depending on the space available.

Briefing questions: What are you going to listen for? How will you know whether your neighbours are inhaling or exhaling? What strategies could you use to help synchronise your breathing (e.g., breathing faster or slower)?

Task: The group lies on the floor, face up in a circle, with their heads in the centre and their bodies radiating out. All members of the group hold hands and shut their eyes. The exercise is to try to breathe in and out at the same time as their neighbour and therefore with all the other members of their group. When this has been achieved the teacher asks the group to breathe in deeply together and then let out their breath slowly together, again doing this in synchronisation.

Debriefing questions: How easy was it to synchronise your normal breathing with one neighbour/two neighbours? What helped? What hindered? Did you get better at it as time went by?

Task 2.5 – I was frightened when . . .

Time: About twenty minutes.

Group size: Pairs (from stable groups – to combine back into stable groups).

Briefing: There might be things that some children cannot talk about. Suggest that they may like to talk about something else that is less frightening. How will you respond if the frightening thing is not frightening to you? Talk about what it means to trust someone.

Task: Carefully pair up children. Children take it in turns to finish the sentence 'I was frightened when . . .' Issues that arise are discussed between paired children. Pairs reverse the order of who goes first and exchange sentences of 'I was happy when . . .' If appropriate, pairs join with another pair to form their stable group and continue the exchange.

Debriefing questions: Was it easier or harder to speak about being happy? As the listener, what skills did you need to use? Are there any other emotions you would be prepared to share with your peers?

Developing trust

PRIMARY

Five activities to develop trust and co-operation between group members.

Resources

All tasks require space such as that in a gym or hall.

Learning objectives

- To develop a sense of trust and co-operation in a group.
- To have fun with other members of the group and class.

Task 3.1 – Trust train

Time: Ten minutes.

Group size: Start in pairs from stable groups and build up, but do not allow the train to become too large and unwieldy.

Briefing: What potential problems might arise in this activity? How can we avoid them? Drivers must not direct the group into potential danger. Everyone (except the driver) must abide by the rule of keeping their eyes shut, and everyone (including the driver) must not run or do anything else that may hurt or harm another. Signals need to be clear and timed ahead. Everyone has a responsibility to pass the signal quickly and accurately. If collisions occur, no one should be blamed.

Task: Pairs stand one behind the other. The child at the back (the driver, with eyes open) rests their hands on the shoulders of the child in front, who has their eyes shut. The driver signals how the train is to move by pressing on the shoulders of the child in front. A press on the left shoulder signals the train is to turn left. A press on the right shoulder signals the train is to turn right. A gentle pull with both hands signals stop. And a gentle press forward means forward. When you add more children to the train, the signals are transmitted down the train from the child at the back to the next child in line. Make journeys around the room, ensuring that the trains do not bump into each other. Change the driver and repeat the exercise until everyone has had a turn as the driver. You could add a course to manoeuvre around for extra fun.

Debriefing questions: Was it easier to be the driver or part of the train? What made it easy or difficult to work together? Did each driver anticipate the direction and speed needed to take the train on a safe journey? What group size was the most manageable? What did you feel about others who did not co-operate? If it was felt that drivers deliberately directed the group into danger, what effect did this have on the trust between group members?

Task 3.2 – Face trust

Time: Ten minutes.

Group size: Pairs of children from their stable groups.

Briefing: What does it mean to trust someone? How can someone lose your trust? How important is it to trust other people in the group/class?

Task: Only use this task if you know that children will behave responsibly, with due attention to health and safety, and check your school's health and safety policy for guidelines on physical contact. Pairs of children stand face to face with their eyes closed. They gently feel their partner's face, hair and neck with their fingertips. You should emphasise that this is best done as quietly and as gently as possible. One variation is that half the children remain with their eyes closed while you provide them with a new partner. Pupils then have to guess through touch alone who that new partner is. You might want to limit the number of pairs doing this at one time to ensure that children act responsibly (e.g., three pairs, with the rest of the class as an audience).

Debriefing questions: How did this exercise make you feel? How easy was it to do the activity? Were you embarrassed? How important is it that we take responsibility for the safety of other people whom we work with?

Task 3.3 – Arches

Time: Ten minutes.

Group size: Pairs of children from their stable groups.

Briefing: As for Task 3.2.

Task: Only use this task if you know that children will behave responsibly, with due attention to health and safety, and check your school's health and safety policy for guidelines. Pairs of children stand facing each other. They hold their arms out straight in front of them and move forward until their fingertips just touch. They should gradually lean forward until their palms are touching and try to find a balance point between partners. If they go too far then they will fall forward. Emphasise to pupils that they should *on no account* allow another person to fall forward. If there are any concerns that this may happen then this activity should not be used. Repeat the activity with another member from their stable group.

Debriefing questions: As for Task 3.2. Also: were you worried that your partner may let you fall?

Task 3.4 – Leaning out

Time: Ten minutes.

Group size: Pairs of children from their stable groups.

Briefing and debriefing: As for Task 3.3.

Task: Only use this task if you know that children will behave responsibly, with due attention to health and safety, and check your school's health and safety policy for guidelines. Pairs of children stand facing each other with their feet touching toe to toe. Pupils link hands or use a safety grip (each person holds on to the wrists of the other – the other person cannot then let go). Children then lean backwards and try to find the balance point. If the balance point is lost then they will begin to fall backwards. Repeat the activity with another member from their stable group.

Task 3.5 – Co-operative letters and shapes

Time: Ten minutes.

Group size: Pairs or fours from their stable groups.

Briefing and debriefing: As for Task 3.3.

Task: Forming letters and shapes may seem simple, but working with a partner requires each child to help and support the other. Groups are asked to form a simple letter, like an 'L' or an 'O'. Progressively the shapes become more complex – 'S', 'M' and 'R'. You can also use simple and complex shapes, from a circle to a parallelogram to a pentagon.

Unit 4

Sensitivity, respect and sharing views

Three activities to develop sensitivity, respect and positivity in the class.

Resources

Photocopy worksheet 4a for Task 4.1 and worksheet 4b for Task 4.2. One sheet per group is needed. Cut up sheets into individual cards.

Learning objectives

* To enhance self-awareness and sensitivity to others' thoughts and feelings.
* To encourage openness, co-operation and the sharing of views between children.

Task 4.1 – Truth game

Time: Twenty minutes.

Group size: Children should work in their stable groups (fours).

Briefing questions: How will you make sure everyone has a go at answering a question? How should you react if someone says something that you do not agree with or you dislike?

Task: Each group places the cards from worksheet 4a face down in the middle of the group. Explain to the groups that members take it in turns to select a card and try to answer the question as truthfully as possible. Other group members should find out why the person answers the way they do. Anyone who feels unable to answer says 'pass' and gives the card to the next person. When all the questions have been answered the pack can be shuffled and they should pick again. Two rounds of this is probably enough. For younger children who have difficulties reading, the teacher can read each question. The idea is to encourage children to explore each other's views and feelings together, and to begin to get to know each other more personally.

Debriefing questions: Which question got 'passed' the most? Were there any questions that no one was willing to answer? Did groups express different views? Did everyone in the group take turns?

Task 4.2 – Predicaments

Time: Twenty minutes to one hour.

Group size: Stable groups (fours).

Briefing: Encourage children to answer the questions as openly as possible, to listen to each other's answers and to ask 'why' questions to get reasons. They could also think about what they should do and then what they actually would do.

Task: Place the pile of prepared cards from Worksheet 4b in the centre of the group.

1   Explain that each person in turn will take a card from the pile. They will read out what is written on the card and then say what they would do in the situation described on the card. If someone does not want to answer a particular card they may say 'pass' and take the next card. The rejected card is placed in the unused pile.

2   The first person takes a card and reads out the predicament, for example 'Your house is on fire. You have time to save two things.' The group can then make comments and a discussion may follow. Keep reminding the group there may be more than one possible answer (and answers are not necessarily correct). Encourage them to explore the reasons given.

3   Continue the process until everyone has had one or more goes. Groups could suggest their own predicaments for other groups to discuss.
    You do not need to use all the cards but, if you don't, make sure you select a range of positive and negative scenarios.

Debriefing questions: How did people answer the question about the person who had collapsed on the pavement? Were they being honest with themselves? Would they really behave like that? What did they learn about themselves? What did they learn about other people? Were some questions harder to discuss than others?

Task 4.3 – 'This week I've noticed that . . .'

Time: Ten to fifteen minutes.

Group size: Whole class, groups or both.

Briefing: Encourage children to think of something nice or positive to say about another person in their group.

Task: Ask children to volunteer to make a positive comment in front of the whole class (or the rest of the group) about another group or classmate. The sentence has to start 'This week I've noticed that . . .' or 'This week I'm pleased that . . .'. Some children will have difficulties in finding a peer to praise. To overcome this you could choose one for them. Teachers should ensure that all children are mentioned. This task can be done on a regular basis at the end of a day or week.

Debriefing: Encourage children to build on these developments. Discuss whether hearing other people say positive things about you affects your confidence. Ensure everyone is included. Encourage pupils to find something positive in difficult situations, such as conflicts or fallings-out.

Worksheet 4a: Sample questions for the truth game

What do you do best?

What sort of TV programmes do you like?

If you won a thousand pounds, what would you spend it on?

What makes you laugh the most?

Who do you like most in the group?

What was your happiest moment?

When was the last time you cried?

What do you think the group needs to do better?

What angered you most last week?

What lie have you told recently?

What scares you the most?

What embarrasses you?

Worksheet 4b: Predicaments

What would you do if . . .?

You are accused of stealing some money by a police officer. You did not do it but you know who did.	While in a supermarket you accidentally knock over a pyramid of cans on display. They go everywhere and everyone is looking.
A friend offers you a stolen video at a very low price.	Someone seems to be following you. There is no one else around.
Your house is on fire. You have time to save two things.	You find a person lying on a busy pavement She could be ill or drunk. Other people are stepping over her.
Someone keeps picking on your best friend.	You see two young men hitting a policeman.
A friend asks you for advice because they have accidentally made a deep scratch with a bike pedal along the side of their dad's brand new car.	You lend five pounds to a friend. Repayment was promised for last Wednesday. Your friend seems to be avoiding you and has not paid back any money.
You have been invited to a friend's birthday party this evening but you also have maths homework that has to be done by tomorrow.	You have one pound to spend in the shop at lunchtime. You can buy yourself either a healthy sandwich or a packet of crisps and a chocolate bar.
You are planning your birthday party and you can have either a clown or a magician, but not both.	Your mum wants you to help her make a cake but your younger sister is having problems with her homework and you can help her understand it. There is only time to do one or the other.
On your birthday you are given a present you already have.	Someone is spreading lies about you.

Unit 5

Becoming a good listener

Resources

Two working ears . . . and Teacher information sheet 5a.

Learning objectives

- To think about what it means to be a good listener.
- To identify what good listening looks and sounds like.
- To practise being a good listener.

Briefing – whole-class work (twenty minutes)

Briefly discuss listening skills, possibly using the following questions:

- Why is it important to listen?
- How does it feel when people do not listen to you?
- How does it feel when people interrupt or talk over you?

Demonstrate poor listening with a child volunteer as the speaker talking about 'What I did at the weekend' and yourself as the listener. Then demonstrate active listening, which might involve:

- engaging with a pupil in a conversation about their favourite sport;
- establishing and maintaining appropriate eye contact;
- nodding and saying 'uh-huh';
- asking clarification questions or for more detail;
- incorporating your own interest in the topic being discussed: for example, 'I used to be a great football player – I really loved it,' then continue discussing your joint interest.

Ask pupils to turn to a partner and discuss the differences between you as poor listener and as active listener, in terms of what you did and did not do (three minutes). Then have a *class discussion* about the two situations. Some questions you might ask:

- What was the difference between the two situations?
- What things indicated/'told you' that I was not listening?
- What did I do when I was actively listening?
- What could [the speaker] have done to make me listen or find out whether I was listening or not?

Group work (ten minutes)

Brainstorm in fours the things people say and do when they are actively listening in a group. Note these in a 'T' chart (see below). Which are the most important ones? The children could also draw up a 'T' chart of poor listening behaviour. Select a scribe for each group to note down the ideas.

Good listener

Sounds like	Looks like
'Uh-huh', 'yes', ask questions, etc.	Maintain eye contact, nod, etc.

Figure 5.1 An example of a 'T' chart

Feedback to the class (five to ten minutes)

Ask two groups to feed back their ideas to the class and note these on a large sheet of paper. Ask other groups whether they came up with any different ideas. Discuss these to ensure they are examples of active listening and narrow down to the five most important in each column (see Teacher information sheet 5a).

Group work – practise listening (fifteen minutes)

In fours, give pupils an opportunity to practise their listening skills. Each group should split into a speaker, two listeners and an observer. The speaker should spend a few minutes talking about one of the topics below. The listeners practise their skills and the observer watches and notes down the listening skills used and how often. After a couple of minutes swap roles to give everyone a turn at practising their listening, speaking and observing skills.

Suggested topics:

- What I like doing in my spare time.
- How I would change the school if I had the chance.
- If I could control all the money in the world I would . . .
- How I would redesign the playground.

Debriefing (ten minutes)

Discuss how easy it was to listen. Did listeners use all the skills identified? Add any new listening skills to the 'T' chart. Discuss what speakers might say to ensure listeners are paying attention and understand what is being said. Encourage children to use their listening skills and to remind each other to use them. *Discuss any rules that pupils would like to add to a list of class rules for group talk.*

Teacher information sheet 5a: Becoming a good listener

Below are some ideas about what makes a good listener. Some of these are more complex than others but, taking into consideration the children in your class, try to ensure that pupils identify most of the following points:

Good listening behaviour:

- Maintaining eye contact, nodding, smiling at the right time, shaking the head at the right time, looking surprised, etc.
- Saying 'yes', 'yeah', 'mm-hm', 'uh-huh', etc.
- Responding – 'Wow', 'That's funny', 'That sounds really great', 'Oh dear', 'Oh really?', 'Right, okay,' 'Cool', 'Hee hee', 'That's interesting', 'Good idea', 'Oh well, 'That's life', etc.
- Asking for clarification – 'I don't understand', 'What do you mean?', 'Which one?', 'How?', 'Why?', 'When?', etc.
- Don't take the focus of the conversation away from the speaker by disagreeing or talking about yourself (unless your point introduces other reasons for being interested in the subject).
- Respond to the feelings that may lie behind the speaker's words. Show that you understand how the speaker feels.
- Don't rush to fill silences. Sit out pauses to encourage the speaker to resume talking.
- Use open-ended questions to encourage the speaker to continue talking or to elaborate.
- Don't 'finish off' what the speaker is saying by interpreting what you think they are trying to say. You might be wrong!

Things speakers can say to ensure someone is listening:

- 'Do you know what I mean?'
- 'Have you ever had that happen to you?'
- 'What do you think?'

LIVERPOOL
JOHN MOORES UNIVERSITY
I.M. MARSH LIBRARY
BARKHILL ROAD
LIVERPOOL L17 6BD
TEL. 0151 231 5216/5299

Unit 6

Listening, asking questions and giving instructions

Learning objectives

- To develop good listening skills.
- To help children to give accurate descriptions.

Briefing – Whole-class work (five minutes)

Ask everyone to think about what they did after school yesterday. All children should be able to recall, but you should encourage pupils to think of three specific things that they did. Put a few examples on the board to stimulate ideas. Encourage children to ask questions of each other. Remind them that there are no right or wrong answers. When finishing the task, each partner should be able to report to the rest of the class one of their partner's activities.

Paired work – three things (ten minutes)

Pairs of children are asked to tell their partner three activities that they did between leaving school yesterday and returning to school today. When one partner completes her/his description, the other relates their three activities. Jointly, the partners should then decide one interesting (or unusual, usual, etc.) activity that each undertook. The teacher then calls the whole class together, and children report on their partner's activity.

Debriefing (five minutes)

With the class, the teacher should emphasise listening and support skills. Discuss how easy it was to listen. Did listeners ask questions? Explore what happened between partners if one of the pair could not remember. How did the pairs decide which one activity to report?

UPPER PRIMARY

Resources

One sheet of paper and a pen for each child. Teacher information sheet 6a. Figures 6.1 to 6.4.

Learning objectives

- To think further about good listening skills.
- To help children give accurate instructions.
- To help children ask relevant questions for clarification.
- To illustrate the effectiveness of two-way communication.

Briefing – Whole-class work (ten minutes)

Recap active listening skills. Make the point that sometimes listeners do not understand and have to ask questions to gain clarification. Emphasise that communication also involves being a good speaker (and listener) and this is important when giving instructions.

Task (ten minutes)

One-way communication task: One child is asked to come to the front to instruct the class in drawing a figure made of squares (Figure 6.1). (Teacher shows only that child the figure.) *The class cannot ask questions or talk to the speaker.* When finished, ask the children to compare what they have drawn with the drawing made by the person next to them. Find out how many people got the drawing right. What were the most common misinterpretations? What could the speaker have done/said to help you understand better? Explain why you have to be explicit.

Two-way communication task: Next, a different child is asked to instruct the class to draw another figure (Figure 6.2). (Teacher shows only that child the figure.) She/he faces the class and the class *may ask questions.* When finished, ask the children to compare what they have drawn with the drawing made by the person next to them. Find out how many people got the drawing exactly right and compare this to the success rate in the one-way task. Ask pairs to think about the differences between the two situations.

Class discussion (ten minutes)

Use Teacher information sheet 6a for discussion. The teacher should note class responses to questions 5 and 6 and save for future reference.

TASKS

The two following activities may be used separately across two sessions or concurrently in one session.

Group work – 'Living sculpture' (ten to fifteen minutes)

Resources: Floor space.

Time: Twenty minutes or more.

Group size: Combine two stable groups together.

Briefing: How will each group decide who will be the leader and the modeller? Listen carefully to the instructions given by the modeller.

Task: (You might want to have a class demonstration of the activity before doing the activity in groups.) The activity requires a modeller and a leader. The modeller is required to sit or stand with his back to the others while they form a standing circle and hold hands. The leader should now give each person a number – 1–7 (or so) – and ask the modeller to shout out action instructions along the lines of: 'No. 4, lift up No. 1's leg'; 'No. 3, put your arm round No. 6's neck'; 'No. 2, crawl through No. 4's legs', etc. The group's hands must remain linked for as long as is humanly possible, and at some point (preferably prior to the collapse of the group in a heap in the middle of the floor!), the modeller should be instructed by the leader to turn round and view the 'living sculpture' he or she has created.

Some 'modellers' may need help in thinking up appropriate instructions and it is important that adult help is offered if ideas do not come spontaneously from the group. The sequence can be repeated several times.

Debriefing: How did it go? What was the hardest part? What made it a success? What could you do next time to make it more successful?

Paired work – 'Escape from Wotu Island' (fifteen minutes)

Resources: Copies of Figures 6.3 for half the class and Figure 6.4 for the other half.

Group size: Pairs from the stable groups.

Scenario: En route to Central America, while flying over the Bermuda Triangle, the engines on your plane cut out. Fortunately, you managed to parachute out of the plane with your radio transmitter before it crashed into the sea. You have floated down and landed in the northern part of a remote island in the middle of the Atlantic Ocean renowned for its inhospitable environment. If the resident crocodiles catch you, they'll certainly eat you! Using your radio, you contact air traffic control and they tell you that they will rescue you from the south of the island, but first you will have to get from the north to the south using the map you have and instructions from the flight controller. The flight controller will guide you around some of the dangerous obstacles in your way. To succeed, all you have to do is stay alive!

Task: Split the class into equal numbers of flight controllers and pilots and then pair them up. Outline the scenario and then give a copy of Figure 6.3 to each pilot and Figure 6.4 to each flight controller. Ask flight controllers and pilots to sit facing each other with a book behind their sheet. *Children must not look at their partner's map.* The flight controller should guide the pilot across the island to the rescue point while avoiding dangerous obstacles. The pilot should draw the route that he/she takes on the map. When they have finished, compare their maps to see if the pilot has survived. Unfortunately, the two maps are old and slightly different from each other: some of the dangers are marked on one map but not on the other. So flight controllers and pilots will need to be very careful and make sure their communication is two way.

Debriefing (ten minutes): Ask the class about:

- the strategies they used to solve the problem;
- the problems they encountered;
- how they clarified what the flight controller meant;
- the sorts of questions that provided useful information; and
- the sorts of descriptions that were most accurate.

How might pupils change their behaviour when helping classmates, based on what they experienced in this exercise? Encourage children to use their listening, questioning and explaining skills when working on activities at other times, for example during class time. *Discuss any rules that pupils would like to add or amend in their list of class rules for group talk.*

Teacher information sheet 6a: Listening, asking questions and giving instructions

1   Which exercise (Figure 6.1 or Figure 6.2) took less time? Why?
2   In which exercise did people *think* they did better? Why do they feel more confident in that exercise?
3   In which exercise did people *actually* do better? Why did more people do better in that exercise?
4   Which exercise was less frustrating for the person giving the instructions? Why wasn't it frustrating for them? Which exercise was less frustrating for those listening? Why?
5   What are the advantages and disadvantages of one-way communication?

Advantages	Disadvantages

6   What are the advantages and disadvantages of two-way communication?

Advantages	Disadvantages

7   How were these exercises like some situations you have been in or seen? Such as: trying to communicate with someone who does not speak your language very well; watching a cookery programme on TV and then trying to make the dish, or following another type of demonstration on TV; trying to follow a teacher's directions.

Source: Farivar and Webb, 1991 (see Useful references, p. 55)

LIVERPOOL JOHN MOORES UNIVERSITY
LEARNING SERVICES

One-way communication

Figure 6.1

Two-way communication

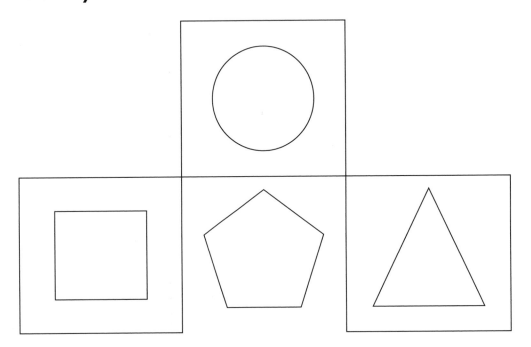

Figure 6.2

Pilot's instructions

- The flight controller will direct you to the rescue point.

- Tell the flight controller about the dangerous obstacles on your map.

- DO NOT LOOK AT THE FLIGHT CONTROLLER'S MAP!

- Draw the route on your map.

- Good luck in your adventure!

You must avoid:

- the quick sand

- Crocodile River

- the haunted forest

- Piranha River

- the bandits

- the bottomless pit

- the volcano

- the pirate village

Figure 6.3 Pilot's map

Flight controller's instructions

- You must direct the pilot to the rescue point.
- Beware of the dangers on your map and on the pilot's map.
- The pilot will tell you what dangerous obstacles are on their map.
- DO NOT LOOK AT THE PILOT'S MAP!
- Good luck in the adventure!

Guide the pilot, but:

- avoid the quick sand
- avoid Crocodile River
- avoid the haunted forest
- avoid Piranha River
- avoid the bandits
- avoid the bottomless pit
- avoid the volcano
- avoid the pirate village

Figure 6.4 Flight controller's map

Helping skills

LOWER PRIMARY

Resources

A4-sized photocopy of rabbit (or similar animal, or an object such as a tree, car, etc.). Enough copies of the rabbit should be made so that each child in the class has one. Each copy of the rabbit is then cut into four random pieces (with older children, it can be cut into a greater number of pieces) so that no two copies of the rabbit are cut into the same pieces. Pieces from two copies of the rabbit are then put into a single envelope (hence thirty rabbits, fifteen envelopes).

Learning objectives

- To think about what it means to be an effective helper/collaborator.
- To understand that sharing resources and ideas is the best way to help.
- To understand that explanations are often important for success and that any individual child cannot simply assert her/his own view.

Briefing – whole-class work (five to ten minutes)

Introduce and explain the lesson objectives above. Remind the pupils of the two lessons that focused on listening skills, asking questions and giving instructions (units 5 and 6). Emphasise the importance of these skills when helping others.

Task (ten to fifteen minutes)

The task can be undertaken in pairs or groups of four. Each pair of children is given an envelope. Whether the children undertake the task in pairs or fours, the teacher asks the children to open the envelope and place the pieces of the rabbit in the centre of the table (where they are sitting). Pairs/groups are then asked to assemble complete pictures of the rabbit.

Debriefing (ten minutes)

Discuss how the children pieced together and shared the construction of the rabbit between partners. What happened if one child tried to dominate the assembly of the rabbits? Did the pairs/groups take turns in choosing pieces? Did the children find it useful talking through their problems? How will they try to help each other in the future? Encourage children to practise and use helping skills during normal class lessons and to remind each other when they are not being helpful. *Discuss any rules that pupils would like to add or amend in their list of class rules for group talk.*

UPPER PRIMARY

Resources

Teacher information sheets 7a and 7b, Worksheets 7c and 7d. Pieces of string for pupils to learn how to tie different types of knot (see Teacher information sheet 7b).

Learning objectives

- To think about what it means to be an effective helper/collaborator.
- To understand that guiding someone through an activity is the best way to help.
- To understand that explanations are often important for success.

Briefing – whole-class work (twenty minutes)

Introduce and explain the lesson objectives above. Remind the pupils of the lesson that focused on clarifying and asking questions, giving feedback and being a good listener (Unit 6). Emphasise the importance of these skills when helping others. Have a short discussion on the following issues:

- What is helping?
- Why do I need to be helped when I can copy?
- When I am helping someone, why can't I just give them the answer, tell them what to do, or do it for them?
- What do we do when we give effective help?

It is important to recognise that helping is also beneficial for the person doing the helping since they must verbalise their thinking in simple ways for the help to be effective. This aids and develops learning and understanding.

In the ensuing discussion two questions you might ask are:

- What things indicated that I was not helping?
- What would I have done if I had been trying to be helpful?

Illustrate through a demonstration and discussion the important distinction between the following different methods of giving help (you could use Teacher information sheet 7b with examples of how to tie a figure of eight knot and a bowline):

- *Showing* someone how to do something before they do the activity: for example, figure of eight knot.
- *Telling* someone how to do something before they do the activity.
- *Guiding* someone through the activity as they do it: that is, telling, showing and explaining as the person works through the activity.

Finally, emphasise the importance (in certain circumstances, such as helping with a maths problem) of the helper asking the person who needs the help to explain what they have done or how they have done something before help is given. This means you can see where the person in need of help has gone wrong.

Paired work – 'explaining problems to each other' (ten to fifteen minutes)

Give half of the class the mathematics problems on Worksheet 7c and the other half those on Worksheet 7d. (If these are too simple or too difficult, pick some other real-life mathematical problems that are more suitable.) After pupils have managed to answer some of the questions, pair them up so that each member of the pair has answered different questions. The pair should take it in turns to explain how to solve one of their problems. Then they should explain to their partner each step in the calculation: what they did first, what they did next and so on. They should not just give the answer ('It's fifty-four') or simplify their methodology ('It's six times nine.').

If problems arise, get pupils to ask their partner how to do the calculation. The pupil in need of help should remember to explain how they tried to do the problem so that the helper can identify where they went wrong. If some children finish more quickly than others, you might like to teach them how to tie a bowline (see Teacher information sheet 7b).

Debriefing (five to ten minutes)

Discuss how easy/hard it was for the children to explain the problems and to break them down for their partners. Did they find it useful talking through the problems? How will they try to help each other in the future? Encourage children to practise and use helping skills during normal class lessons and to remind each other when they are not being helpful. *Discuss any rules that pupils would like to add or adjust in their list of class rules for group talk.*

Follow-up work

Another way to integrate helping alongside more collaborative work is as follows:

1   Pupils devise problems (possibly maths problems) in pairs.
2   Pass problems to the next pair along the line, who try to solve them.

3   Pass problems back to the original pair for marking.

4   One member from each pair explains to one member from the next pair where that pair went wrong (presuming that they did go wrong!).

5   The pairs reform and the one child explains to their partner where they went wrong.

Teacher information sheet 7a: Being a good helper

Below are some ideas about what being a good helper 'looks like' and 'sounds like'. Some of these are more complex than others, but taking into consideration the children in your class, try to ensure that pupils identify most of the following points:

Good helping behaviour:

- Notice when others need help (look around in your group and see if anyone might need help).
- Tell others to ask you if they need help.
- When someone asks you for help, help them.
- Encourage the person to explain what they have done so far or how they did it.
- Be a good listener: let the person explain what help they need.
- Do not give the answer or do the task for the person; rather, guide them through it.
- Give explanations so that the person understands why they should do something in a particular way.
- Watch while the person tries to do the task themself; guide them if necessary.
- Give specific feedback on how the problem/task was tackled.
- Praise the person when they have tried and succeeded in doing the task.
- Check they have understood why this was the best way to solve the problem.

Things helpers can say to make sure people who need help know they are willing to assist:

- 'If you need help, ask me.'
- 'Of course I'll help you. What help do you need?'
- 'Tell me what you've done so far.'
- 'How did you do this?'
- 'Let me explain the way I would do this.'
- 'Why don't you have a go now and I'll watch you do it.'
- 'You got up to this part right. Now this is where you went wrong.'
- 'Well done, I think you've got it!'
- 'Tell me how you would do this the next time.'
- 'You're a star!'

Teacher information sheet 7b: Helping skills

If you are not familiar with these knots, it is advisable to pracise them a few times first.

The figure of eight knot

1 First make a loop in front of you
2 Put your hand behind and through the back of the loop so that you can see the pads of your fingers and palm.
3 Twist your hand so your fingers move away from you. Now you see your fingernails. Grab hold of the end of the string and pull it through the loop.
4 You now have a figure of eight knot.

If you double the string up from the start, you can make it so that you have a loop at the end.

The bowline

The bowline (pronounced 'bo-lin') is a really handy knot because of its great strength and the ease with which it can be undone, even when it has been put under great tension. It also does not slip. It can be used in lots of different situations: climbers, sailors and firemen all use this knot. The only drawback is that it is difficult to learn how to tie when using the traditional method. Try this version instead:

1 Create a 'rabbit hole' as in the diagram. Pass the end of the rope around (or through) the object being tied to (marked as x).
2 The 'rabbit' (the end of the string) then comes out of its 'hole', goes around the 'tree' (the string furthest, and leading away, from the object being tied to), then back into its 'hole'.
3 You now have a bowline knot

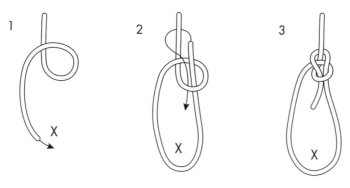

Worksheet 7c: Real-life maths problems

When working out the answers, think about what you do first, second and so on until you have completed the problem.

1   There are twelve sweets in each packet. How many sweets are there in six packets?

2   Brian has four CD towers. Each tower has thirty-five CDs. How many CDs does Brian have in total?

3   Harjeet has read one-eighth of her magazine. She has read to page twelve. How many pages does her magazine have?

Worksheet 7d: Real-life maths problems

When working out the answers, think about what you do first, second and so on until you have completed the problem.

1   Clare is twenty-seven. Her mother is nineteen years older. How old is Clare's mother?

2   Three-quarters of the thirty-two people in a supermarket are adults. How many are children?

3   Tariq has read to page fifty-four of his book. He needs to read twenty-one more pages to reach halfway. How many pages does Tariq's book have?

Group discussion

Giving reasons and weighing up ideas

LOWER PRIMARY

Learning objectives

- To help children understand that they need to give reasons that underlie their ideas.
- To help children understand that they need to weigh up the reasons and evidence for and against an idea.
- To encourage children to practise giving and asking for reasons.

Briefing (five to ten minutes)

Introduce and explain the lesson objectives and emphasise the importance of speaking and listening in relation to explanations and giving reasons. Refer children back to previous group-work tasks where they have had to make decisions.

Group work (ten to fifteen minutes)

Working in pairs, children are asked where they might like to go for a class visit. The pairs should be encouraged to make a short list (between two and four) of places to visit. When the children have put together their lists, each pair should then say why the class might like to visit each of the places. If there is time, the teacher can encourage each pair to choose one 'best' place to visit, and explain why they made this choice. Following these discussions, a whole-class session can be used to identify the range of places to visit.

Debriefing (five to ten minutes)

Review with the class how they came to identify the range of class visits. Then ask the children to review whether it was difficult to provide reasons for each visit. Ask the children to reflect on why it is important to give reasons for choices and suggestions.

UPPER PRIMARY

Resources

Teacher information sheet 8a is primarily for your benefit, but the phrases can be discussed with pupils.

Learning objectives

- To help children understand why they need to give reasons for ideas and the importance of weighing up the reasons and evidence for and against an idea.
- To encourage children to practise giving and asking for reasons and to think about evidence for and against ideas.

Briefing – whole-class work (ten minutes)

Introduce and explain the lesson objectives and recap about speaking and listening in relation to explanations and giving reasons. Refer children back to previous group-work tasks where they have had to make decisions. In these situations children were encouraged to give reasons for their ideas. Ask the children to think back to how and why this was useful and then discuss the following:

- What reasons are.
- Why it is important that we give reasons.
- What we say when we give and ask for reasons during group discussion (see Teacher information sheet 8a).
- What giving reasons helps us to do.

Explain that, when discussing an issue, giving reasons and weighing up the evidence for *and against* an idea helps others understand how we see things and helps us to make better decisions and solve problems.

Group work – having a debate (thirty-five minutes or longer – see Follow-up work)

This task is complex, so you are advised to break it down into stages. In this way, the pupils will be able to focus on what they are doing at the moment, rather than on the complexities of what they will have to do next. You should emphasise to pupils that you hope to hear them using some of the phrases listed on Teacher information sheet 8a during their discussions throughout the activity.

- Step 1 (ten minutes): Split the class into equal numbers of pairs. Select one (or more) of the controversial topics listed below. Half of the pairs are to identify three (or more) opinions and their associated reasons in favour of the statement; the other half a similar number of opinions and associated reasons against the statement. The pairs should note down their arguments.
- Step 2 (fifteen minutes): Combine pairs that are 'for' with those that are 'against' to form groups of four. These groups then report their arguments to each other and discuss them, trying to find ways to counter each other's arguments. They should note down any criticisms next to the ideas they came up with.
- Step 3 (ten minutes): Ask the groups to have a full discussion to decide on the correctness of the statement and to note the reasons why they reached the conclusion they did. If pupils are not able to decide after ten minutes, allow them to agree to disagree (you may be there a long time otherwise!).

Choose from the following controversial topics:

- Hunting foxes is inhumane
- Zoos are good places for animals
- Being in the circus is a good life for both humans and animals

- Dropping litter keeps people in a job
- Recycling is a good thing
- Saving energy is a waste of time
- Watching horror movies makes people more violent
- Children should be allowed to stay up late to watch TV
- Playing violent console games makes people more aggressive

Debriefing questions

- How well did they report arguments for and against ideas?
- When they discussed the arguments for and against, did they feel as though they were going around in circles?
- Did they find that this helped them weigh up alternative ideas more successfully?
- Were the groups able to agree on whether the original statement was correct?
- How did they resolve disputes? Did they have to agree to disagree?
- How would they do things differently next time?

Encourage pupils to give reasons for their thinking and explanations when doing group work in other lessons. *Discuss any rules that pupils would like to add or amend in their list of class rules for group talk.*

Follow-up work

After the debate activity each group could compile a report exploring some of the arguments for and against, and the criticisms of these arguments.

Groups could devise and perform a simple role-play scene where the arguments for and against are acted out or explored.

The views on the controversial topic could be prepared as speeches or articles for a newspaper in a persuasive, evaluative or informative format.

Teacher information sheet 8a: Phrases often used to provide reasoning during group work

Sounds like	Communicative action
'Why?'	Requests reason
'Maybe . . . because . . .'	Suggestion plus reason
'How about . . . because . . .'	Suggestion plus reason
'I think . . . because . . .'	Opinion plus reason
'No, that can't be right because . . . so . . .'	Exploring implications of an argument.
'If . . . then . . .'	Exploring reasoning
'Yes . . . but . . .'	Giving reasons against an idea
'No . . . because . . .'	Giving reasons against an idea
'But what about . . .?'	Raising alternative interpretations
'I understand your point of view but . . .'	Raising alternative interpretations
'I can see why you think that is a good idea but consider this . . .'	Raising alternative interpretations

Group discussion

Making suggestions and speculating

Resources

For each group class teachers will need one large sheet of drawing (or writing) paper and enough pencils for each member of the group. The task described below is known as 'co-operative drawing', so children will need space to lay out their paper to undertake any drawing.

Learning objectives

- To encourage children to use and think about reasons and reasoning in talk.
- To think about the process of making suggestions and speculating.
- To encourage children to practise making suggestions and speculating.

Briefing (five to ten minutes)

Introduce and explain the lesson objectives and emphasise the importance of considering what can be drawn, agreeing who will draw what on the paper, and considering alternative objects to draw. Refer back to previous work on giving reasons for and against ideas, making suggestions and speculating. Remind children that when they have worked on group-work tasks they have often had to make group decisions.

Group work (fifteen minutes)

Give pairs (later this can be undertaken in small groups) one sheet of paper and two pencils. Ask them to make a drawing related to a current classroom topic (Tudor house, mini-beasts/insects, etc.). Before each pair begins the drawing, however, suggest that they agree what to draw and (perhaps) who should do which part of the drawing. As children become more competent with this activity, you can introduce colour and more complicated objects to draw.

Debriefing questions (five to ten minutes)

- How well did the pairs work together?
- Were they able to agree what to draw?
- Did they make suggestions about to what to draw?

LIVERPOOL
JOHN MOORES UNIVERSITY
I.M. MARSH LIBRARY
BARKHILL ROAD
LIVERPOOL L17 6BD
TEL. 0151 231 5216/5299

UPPER PRIMARY

Resources

Worksheet 9a and Teacher information sheet 9b.

Learning objectives

- To encourage children to use and think about reasons and reasoning in talk.
- To think about the process of making suggestions and speculating.
- To encourage children to practise making suggestions and speculating.

Briefing – whole-class work (fifteen to twenty minutes)

Introduce and explain the lesson objectives and then recap what the class did in the lesson on giving reasons and weighing up ideas (Unit 8). Tell pupils that another important skill in group work is to be able to suggest alternative ideas and to speculate as to why something may be the case.

- Suggestions (five to ten minutes): When we engage in *brainstorming* the point is to come up with lots of different *possible* ideas. These ideas are only suggestions, and we may decide that some are better than others. Carry out a brainstorming session asking for suggestions for the following scenario: 'We have been given ten pounds by our headteacher. What shall we spend the money on?' Ask pupils to make suggestions about how the money could be spent. Emphasise that we all have our personal preferences and we could argue for ever, but the idea is to try to find something that we all might like. Encourage more tentative suggestions rather than definite advice/opinions. For example, encourage pupils to say, 'Maybe . . .', 'You could . . .' 'How about . . .?', rather than 'I think . . .', 'We will . . .', 'We should . . .' You could finish off the activity by requesting reasons for and against the different ideas and then conclude with a vote.
- Speculating (five to ten minutes): Speculating is more about finding explanations for why something *might* happen – we use these in science. You could ask your pupils to speculate about one or two of the following questions (it does not matter if they are right or wrong – just get them to give an explanation.):
    - Why can we see stars only when it is dark or nearly dark?
    - Why does the moon seem to change shape?
    - Why do we see the moon only when it is dark or nearly dark?
    - If the world is round, why don't people at the bottom fall off?
    - Do people in Australia see everything upside down?

Group work – 'Lost in space' (fifteen minutes)

In their stable groups of four, two children in each group should take on the roles of scribe and chairperson (to ensure everyone presents their ideas and provides reasons). The others have a main responsibility for coming up with ideas and developing them.

Distribute a copy of Worksheet 9a to the scribe in each group and ask them to read out the scenario to the group. Groups must decide which five items they would save from the wreckage of the space-ship before it explodes. *Everyone in the group must have an opportunity to suggest and speculate*; it is up to the chairperson to enforce this. The group should consider each item in turn and discuss the evidence for and against saving it. The scribe could make notes on a piece of scrap paper. The scribe in each group should note down on Worksheet 9a the five items that the group finally decide they will save and the reasons why. The group should also decide what else it should do: for example, remain where it is or attempt to reach the space camp.

When each group has finished, the class should discuss the ideas and reasons for and against saving each item from the wreckage. A class answer should be sought and then compared to that suggested by NASA experts (see Teacher information sheet 9b).

Debriefing questions (five to ten minutes)

* How well did they get on with making suggestions and speculating? Did this help?
* Did they report reasons for and against these ideas?
* Did they find that this helped them make better decisions?
* How did you resolve disputes?
* How would you do things differently next time?

Encourage children to practise and use making suggestions and speculating during normal class lessons. *Discuss any rules that pupils would like to add or amend in their list of class rules for group talk.*

Worksheet 9a: Lost in space

You were in a space-ship travelling to the moon. Unfortunately, the space-ship has malfunctioned and crash-landed on the moon. You and your group are the only people to survive. It will take five days for Mission Control to prepare and send another space-ship to rescue you. There is a space camp six days' walk away. A couple of you have severe limb injuries but fortunately your space-suits and air-tanks (with a day's supply of air) are undamaged.

Your space-ship is still on fire and is going to blow up. There is just time for you to save five things from this list of twelve items. You must decide as a group which items you are going to save. If you make the right decisions, you will survive. If you don't, you will perish!

- 1 box matches
- 1 tube food concentrate
- 1 portable gas heater
- 2 pistols
- 1 diet orange drink
- 1 telecommunications system (receiver and transmitter with solar batteries)
- 1 first-aid box
- 2 oxygen cylinders (ten litres in each)
- 1 compass
- five litres water
- 3 signal flares (usable in a vacuum)
- 1 map of the moon

The chairperson must ensure that everyone has an opportunity and is encouraged to present their view. The scribe should note down the five items that the group decides to save and the reasons why these are so important.

- The most important item to save is ....

  because ....

  ....

- The second important item to save is ....

  because ....

  ....

- The third important item to save is ....

  because ....

  ....

- The fourth important item to save is ....

  because ....

  ....

- The fifth important item to save is ....

  because ....

  ....

Teacher information sheet 9b: Lost in space

Groups should decide to remain where they are as it will take longer to walk to the camp than for a rescue shuttle to arrive. Also, they do not know what dangers they may face on the long walk, which will be very difficult anyway as some of them are injured. The group might decide to split up, with the healthy members walking to the camp and the injured ones remaining at the crash site. This is not recommended since it will be very difficult for any rescue mission to find them if they get lost or stuck.

The list below shows how important each object is for survival, according to NASA experts. To see how well the class has done, the points allocated to each object can be totalled by the teacher. Anything above 0 means they survive. (It may not be a good idea to total the points for each group as this may result in conflict between groups and some bragging that they are doing better than others.)

1	Oxygen cylinders – there is no air in space	5
2	Water – there is no water on the moon	5
3	First-aid box – to treat injuries from the crash	3
4	Food concentrate – there is no food on the moon	2
5	Telecommunication system – to communicate with Mission Control, to explain where you are and what has happened	2
6	Signal flares – to signal your location to rescuers	1
7	Map of the Moon – might help you tell your rescuers where you are if you also have telecommunication system, although they would probably know better than you, since rockets are tracked	0
8	Pistols – what are you going to shoot (apart from each other when you are starving)?	–2
9	Diet orange drink – has few nutrients	–2
10	Heater – you are in a vacuum so the gas would not ignite, and you are wearing space-suits so you will not get cold	–2
11	Compass – there is no magnetic north on the moon	–2
12	Matches – you are in a vacuum so the match will not light	–2

Group decisions

Reaching a consensus

Resources

For each group teachers will need either a real (small) bag of sweets or a chocolate bar. Alternatively, you could photocopy (for each group) a bag of sweets or a chocolate bar. If you photocopy the bag of sweets, ensure that the number of sweets is identified on the bag or write the number on the photocopy.

Learning objectives

- To think about the process of making group decisions by reaching a consensus.
- To practise making group decisions through consensus.

Briefing (five to ten minutes)

Introduce and explain the lesson objectives and emphasise the importance of speaking and listening in relation to explanations and giving reasons. Refer back to the previous work on giving reasons for and against ideas, making suggestions and speculating. Remind children that when they have worked on group-work tasks they have often had to make group decisions. Making these decisions is not always easy but looking at the reasons for and against ideas helps the group make a decision.

Group work (ten minutes)

Working in pairs or small groups, each group is given a bag of sweets or a chocolate bar (or the photocopy). The children are asked how they can divide the sweets/chocolate among the group members. Groups may be encouraged to undertake a 'fair' distribution or agree another method of distribution. After each group has agreed a means of distribution, call the class back together and ask each group to report on their distribution. (It is optional whether you then allow the children to distribute and eat the sweets!)

Debriefing (five to ten minutes)

Review with the class how they came to distribute the sweets/chocolate. Then ask children to review whether it was difficult to decide on the means to distribute the sweets. Ask them to reflect on why it is important to give reasons for choices and suggestions.

Follow-up

If the discussion concerning distribution is too easy for the groups, try to find another object of 'value' to the children that may not be divided by a simple mathematical distribution (such as five sweets between four children) and ask them to undertake the discussion for distribution task.

UPPER PRIMARY

Resources

Worksheets 10a to 10d.

Learning objectives

- To think about the process of making group decisions by reaching a consensus.
- To practise making group decisions through consensus.

Briefing – Whole-class work (twenty minutes)

Go over the learning objectives. Refer back to the previous work on giving reasons for and against ideas, making suggestions and speculating. Remind children that when they have worked on group-work tasks they have often made group decisions. Making these decisions is not always easy but looking at the reasons for and against ideas helps the group make a decision. This is done by finding the most sensible or logical reasons.

Discuss with your class the different ways of making decisions – voting by hand-raising, private balloting and just asking if anyone disagrees/everyone agrees. In which situations would we use these and when would they be unsuitable? (Think about the number of people involved, the seriousness of the decision, the amount of money and time it might cost, the context etc.) What are the problems with each form of reaching consensus? For example, a private ballot is time-consuming and expensive. Public voting is formal and encourages conformity (especially if the question is hard, such as 'Who thinks the square root of 169 is 13?'). Asking if any-one disagrees is informal and encourages people to offer their view but only in small, familiar group situations (imagine a teacher asking the pupils this during assembly!).

Discourage pupils from voting when in small groups (this should be reserved for class discussion, etc.). Rather, they should make sure they have discussed the issues fully and that everyone has had an opportunity to have their say. Emphasise that when working in their groups they should always check that everyone has had a chance to say what they think and time to consider the issues. The phrases you can use to check that everyone is in agreement might be 'Are we all agreed?' or 'Can anyone think of a good reason why we shouldn't do/choose this?'

Group work – 'Best pet' (ten minutes)

In groups of four, use the information (see Worksheet 10a) to make decisions about which pet matches which owner. Groups should decide what should be done with the remaining pet. Upper primary pupils could prepare a case arguing why that pet should not be put down.

Group work – 'Best holiday' (ten minutes)

In groups of four, use the information (see Worksheet 10b) to make decisions about which holiday matches which person. Groups should outline their reasoning for each choice.

Group work – 'Who should be the class representative?' (twenty minutes)

In groups of four, use the information (see Worksheets 10c and 10d) to make a decision about which of the four pupils should be the class representative on the school council. Pupils should discuss the alternatives and then think about the criteria to use to select someone (e.g., ability to work with others, public speaking, being persuasive, confident).

Remind groups to use the ground rules for talk, to give reasons and counter-reasons to help weigh up the alternative arguments. Groups may need to identify who will be spokesperson.

Debriefing questions (ten minutes or so)

* Who did they decide should become the class representative and for what reason?
* What criteria did they use for remaking this decision?
* Did they all agree?
* What did they do if they could not all agree?
* Did all groups suggest the same person? Why not?
* Do you think the class teacher will be pleased with your decisions? Why?
* Could a compromise decision be reached (e.g., sharing the position)?

Group work – 'Group debate' (ten minutes)

Your headteacher has been given some money to redevelop the playground but wants pupils to decide how the money should be spent. It can be spent on only one of the following:

* building a wall down the middle of the playground so that the boys and girls can have separate play areas, and so that balls can be bounced against the wall;
* putting a roof on the playground so that it is always dry and warm; or
* planting a hedge to encourage birds, animals and insects back into the area and making a quiet area.

In fours, discuss which approach (questionnaire, debate, vote, survey) should be used to decide how the money should be spent. If two ideas are equally popular, how will this be resolved? Will it depend on cost, value for money or something else? The groups could also try to reach a consensus on one of the options for the playground. Are these good ideas? Are there better ones? A group spokesperson summarises the discussion and decision-making.

Debriefing

Ask groups/pairs to evaluate how well they worked as a group and how they could improve on their group work if necessary (two minutes). Ask the class to evaluate how well they got on in terms of the particular skill discussed during the briefing. Do they have any new insights or strategies for how better to deal with this problem, etc.? Encourage children to practise making decisions during normal class lessons. *Discuss any rules that pupils would like to add or amend in their list of class rules for group talk.*

Worksheet 10a: Best pet

- A GP, often on call, wants a pet that is low maintenance, tranquil and soothing.

- A taxi-driver doing shift work who likes learning about new things and collecting.

- A checkout worker who has asthma and eczema and has to keep dust levels low at home.

- An only child who needs bringing out of herself and wants a pet to share her worries and fears with.

Parrot

Exotic fish

Cat

Dalmation dog

Pot-bellied pig

Worksheet 10b: Best holiday

- Retired widower who wants companionship and intellectual stimulation. Has a fear of flying but no time or cost limits.
- Single university student on a tight budget. Wants a good night-life and likes to be active.
- Young newly-weds. Want late honeymoon in a romantic, exotic setting. Price limit because they've just bought a house, but want comfort and something memorable.
- Couple in their late thirties with twin teenage boys. Limited resources but must have a Saturday night away and no extra expenses. Boys like skate-boarding; man likes looking at birds through his binoculars; woman wants to collapse by a pool with a good paperback.

Ski-resort: Ante- and après-ski facilities (bars, cafés, clubs). All-in price, including hire of skis and ski passes. Spa hotel nearby where you can spend a day in Turkish steam rooms, have seaweed packs and massage.

Archaeological tour: Have to be fairly fit because the tour includes a lot of walking to sites that are inaccessible by coach. Price includes all meals but it is expensive. Field-notes sent before and background reading list given.

Cruise: Coach leaves from central London and meets ship at Dover. Route into the Baltic stopping at Riga, Tallinn, St Petersburg and Helsinki. Ship has hairdressers, swimming pools, cabaret and other entertainment, as well as kids' clubs, amusement arcade and quiz nights. All meals included but will need spending money aboard and ashore.

Club Mediterranean: Extinct volcanic island with camp on it. Basic accommodation, but lots of watersports: windsurfing, paragliding, water-skiing, snorkelling. Food included but not the extra activities.

Worksheet 10c: Who should be the class representative?

It is the beginning of another term and the headteacher of Ferryboat School has decided to set up a school council. The problem is that the teachers know that there are many children in their classes who would *enjoy* being the class representative but who might not be the *best pupil* to communicate the class's opinion on school matters. One teacher, Miss Langrick, has asked you to help her make this difficult decision. After a vote, the following *four* pupils had the same number of votes. She needs to choose just *one* person from the candidates.

You must decide which pupil should be the class representative and explain why. You should also explain why the others should not be given the responsibility. When you have made a decision, complete the sentences below for each of the four children.

.... should not be made class representative

because ....

....

....

.... should not be made class representative

because ....

....

....

.... should not be made class representative

because ....

....

....

.... should be made class representative

because ....

....

....

Worksheet 10d: The candidates

Javid is a popular boy with many friends, mainly other boys. He likes to be the focus of attention and likes to get his own way. He is confident and good at speaking in front of a large audience. He is fairly good at group work but sometimes he ignores what the girls have to say and he is not very good at persuading people. He wants to be the class representative because it will mean he can miss lessons.

Maria is also popular, and has a mix of boy and girl friends. She likes to play a leading role without dominating other children and is good at working with others and persuading them. She is very conscious of the fact that she has a lisp. When she has to read out her work to the class her voice becomes very quiet, even though her writing is usually very interesting and she has good ideas. She doesn't want to be the class representative but her friends put her forward.

Aran is a very able boy who thinks a lot about things that are happening in the world. He has a few friends in the class. He is quiet in lessons and likes to get on with tasks on his own, although he can work well in a group. He is not a natural leader but when there are problem-solving tasks in science and maths he usually finds the best way to solve them. He is not bothered about being the class representative.

Raksha has one good friend, another girl, and they spend all their time together. They always want to sit next to each other and work together. They won't let other children play their games or share their secrets. But Raksha desperately wants to be the class representative. She is very confident but does not listen to what other people have to say, so few people listen to her.

More decision-making

Consensus and compromise

Resources

Worksheets 11a, 11b and 11c.

Learning objectives

- To think about the process of making group decisions by reaching a consensus.
- To think about the process of making compromise decisions during group work when a unanimous decision cannot be reached.
- To practise making group decisions through consensus.

Briefing – whole-class work (ten minutes)

Explain the learning objectives. Refer back to previous work on giving reasons, suggestions and coming to a consensus. Explore pupils' feelings about how easy or hard they found it in previous lessons to reach a consensus so that a decision could be made. If they found reaching a consensus difficult, explore ways in which they could overcome this problem. Get pupils to anticipate how they will deal with conflict if it arises.

Group work – 'Who should get the pay rise?' (fifteen minutes)

Put pupils into groups of four or six (an even number so that there is no easy majority) and give them Worksheet 11a. The groups should decide which employee should receive the pay rise. First they should think about the criteria to use to select someone. Give the groups ten to fifteen minutes to discuss the problem until they think they have made a decision. Remind the groups to use the ground rules for talk and remember to give reasons and counter-reasons to help weigh up the alternative arguments.

Group feedback (five minutes)

- Who did pupils decide should get the pay rise and for what reason?
- What criteria did they use for making a decision?
- Did all groups suggest the same person? Why not?
- Do you think the company will be pleased with your decision? Why?
- If a compromise was reached, would it be acceptable? For example, could the pay rise be shared between several employees?

Debriefing (five to ten minutes)

Ask children how easy it was to reach group decisions. Explore the different ways groups achieved (or failed to achieve) a consensus decision. Did they all discuss the reasons for and against the different ideas? What did they do when they could not agree? Did they have to come to a compromise? How did they do this? Encourage children to remember the successful decision-making strategies and to try to use them in the future when making decisions and resolving disagreement. *Discuss any rules that pupils would like to add or amend in their list of class rules for group talk.*

Follow-up work

Groups could consider the criteria they used to decide who should get the pay rise. Alternatively, they could identify a number of criteria – good at their work, have good ideas, problems at home, etc. – put ticks in the boxes, decide which criteria are the most important from different perspectives – the employer's, welfare, etc. – and then re-evaluate who should get the pay rise.

Group work – 'Floating and sinking' (fifteen minutes)

Give pupils individual worksheet 11b and ask them to predict individually whether the different items will float or sink. After a few minutes put them into groups of four and ask them to compare their predictions. (Remind the groups that they should use the ground rules for group talking and remember to provide reasons.) Give each group Worksheet 11c and ask members to reach a consensus on which objects will float and their reasons why. Ask the groups to choose a spokesperson who will summarise their joint decision and reasons.

Groups that finish early might like to predict whether the objects would sink or float if the water is heated, if salt/oil is added to the water, if sugar is added to the water, or if the water is replaced with honey.

Give pupils the opportunity to test their predictions and then to reconvene as a group to explain where they went wrong and explore the reasons why.

Worksheet 11a: Who should get the pay rise?

The Smelly Crisps Company has made a large profit this year since it introduced its new brand of sock-flavoured crisps. The board of directors has agreed that some of their staff should get a salary increase to reward them for their work. The problem is that they cannot decide which of four workers should be given the pay rise. They have decided to ask you to help them make this difficult decision.

Paul is a fifty-year-old man, married with two children who are aged twenty and twenty-two. He has worked for the company for thirty years. He is the marketing manager and receives a high salary already. His work is not brilliant but not bad either.

Meena is a 30-year-old woman, married with one child at nursery. She has worked for the company for five years and does the company accounts. Her salary is high. She often arrives late but her work is brilliant.

Amir is a twenty-two-year-old man, unmarried with one five-year-old child. He has worked for the company for two years and it was his idea to produce the new sock-flavoured crisps. His job is to ensure quality control. Recently he has made a bad impression on management by making critical comments. His work is average.

Helen is a nineteen-year-old woman, unmarried with one child. She also looks after her ill mother. She has worked for the company for six months, packing the crisp packets into boxes when they come off the conveyer belt. Her work and attendance are poor.

You must decide which person should get the pay rise and explain why. You should also explain why the others should not be given the pay rise. When you have made a decision, complete the sentences below for each of the 4 people.

.... **should not** be given the pay rise because

....

....

.... **should not** be given the pay rise because

....

....

.... **should not** be given the pay rise because

....

....

.... **should** be given the pay rise because

....

....

Individual worksheet 11b: Floating and sinking

Pretend there is a tank of water in front of you. Which of the following objects would float and which would sink? Explain the reasoning behind your answers.

	Float	Sink	Because . . .
A flat metal pencil case will			....
A metal toy truck will			... ...
A plastic bottle will			... ...
A plastic ruler will			... ...
A wooden tray will			... ...
A wooden chopstick will			... ...

Worksheet 11c: Floating and sinking

Which objects do you, as a group, think will float? And which do you think will sink? For each object, go around the group and find out what each person wrote when they completed the sheet individually. Talk about the reasons you gave for your individual predictions and come up with an agreed group prediction, and why you think the objects will float or sink. The scribe should record these below.

We predict that a flat metal pencil case will float/sink because ....

....

....

We predict that a metal toy truck will float/sink because ....

....

....

We predict that a plastic bottle will float/sink because ....

....

....

We predict that a plastic ruler will float/sink because ....

....

....

We predict that a wooden tray will float/sink because ....

....

....

We predict that a wooden chopstick will float/sink because ....

....

....

Unit 12

Roles within group work

Resources

Pens, paper, Worksheets 12b and 12c, and Teacher information sheet 12a.

Learning objectives

- To get pupils thinking about the various roles or special jobs they can take on when working in a group.
- To get pupils thinking about what different roles might entail.
- To get pupils thinking about how they perform different roles.
- To give pupils practice in performing roles.

Briefing and introduction – whole-class work (ten minutes)

Explain that in some group-work activities it is helpful if group members take on special roles to help in accomplishing the task. Discuss the lesson objectives and the following questions:

- What different roles or special jobs might be used during group work?
- What do these roles or special jobs involve?

Here are some suggestions for the roles that might be used most often:

- Chairperson/manager/organiser/co-ordinator
- Scribe/note-taker/secretary
- Time-keeper
- Supporter/praiser/encourager
- Observer/evaluator
- Spokesperson

There may also be other roles that are particular to the activity: for example, responsibility for organising transport, organising equipment or picnic-maker for a school outing.

Remind pupils that a group should use roles only when they are absolutely necessary. Roles such as opinion-seeker, information-giver, ideas person, explanation-seeker, tension-releaser and so on are all roles that all group members should be adopting all the time, and thus do not need to be specifically designated.

Group activity – role descriptions (ten to fifteen minutes)

It is important that pupils have a clear sense about what is involved in carrying out the role and also how to take on the role in practice in terms of what might be said and done.

Organise pupils into small groups of three or four. Allocate each group one of four roles to discuss. The group should identify a job description for their role and list this on a single sheet of paper. (Note: these could be referred to by other pupils in the future when taking on that role.) At this point teachers may decide that a debriefing is necessary before ending the lesson or continuing with the remaining tasks which may be best covered on another day.

Preparation for electric circuits/insulators work (five to ten minutes)

Use the same groups as in the previous task. Outline what the groups will have to do in relation to the task below and ask the pupils to come up with some ideas as to how they would perform their role in terms of what they might say and do according to their job descriptions. These could be listed in a 'T' chart on a sheet of paper (see p. 74).

Repeat this exercise prior to doing the tasks on electricity/insulators to identify a different approach to performing the role in a different context.

Group work – electric circuits, conductors and insulators (ten to fifteen minutes)

The objective is to give pupils experience of carrying out their roles in a different type of task. Children should remain in the groups used for the previous discussion task.

Allow pupils five minutes to discuss and plan how they will perform their roles before giving them the materials to start doing their task.

Depending on the previous experience of your class in this area, give pupils either the task of predicting whether the bulb will light up (Worksheet 12b) or the task of predicting whether certain materials act as insulators or conductors (Worksheet 12c).

Debriefing (five to ten minutes)

Discuss pupils' answers and explanations. Ask pupils how they got on with their roles. Identify a few examples of how children carrying out each role put that role into practice. Did they do things differently from in the previous task? What did they say and do? Did they find it difficult to do their role and contribute to the group discussion at the same time? Did anyone find that they could not perform their role because they were too involved in the group discussion? Any thoughts on how they could perform their role better in future?

Follow-up work

Encourage groups to think about whether they need to take on roles, which roles are useful and which they are not good at performing. This could be part of a discussion about how pupils can further improve their group-working skills.

LIVERPOOL JOHN MOORES UNIVERSITY
LEARNING SERVICES

Teacher information sheet 12a: Key to circuitry symbols

1 Battery or cell	
2 Batteries	
Wire	
Lamp	
Closed switch (on)	
Open switch (off)	

Answers to 'Working circuits' diagrams

The bulbs in Diagrams 1, 4 and 6 will be lit. Diagrams 2 and 3 have no battery. In Diagram 5 the switch is off.

Answers to 'Insulators and conductors'

Wood, plastic and rubber all act as insulators. Metal and water conduct electricity.

Worksheet 12b: Working circuits

Look at each of the circuit diagrams. Do you think the bulb(s) are alight? Complete the sentences by crossing out the answer that is wrong and writing in the reason for your group answer.

   Make sure you find out what each person in your group thinks. Talk about your reasons. Make sure you come to an agreed **group** answer and reason why you think the bulb(s) will be alight or not.

1   We think the bulb is alight/not
     alight because
     ....
     ....

2   We think the bulbs are alight/not
     alight because
     ....
     ....

3   We think the bulb is alight/not
     alight because
     ....
     ....

4   We think the bulb is alight/not
     alight because
     ....
     ....

5   We think the bulb is alight/not
     alight because
     ....
     ....

6   We think the bulbs are alight/not
     alight because
     ....
     ....

Worksheet 12c: Insulators and conductors

An easy way to test whether materials are conductors or insulators is to use this circuit.

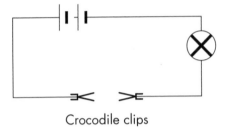

Crocodile clips

Attach the crocodile clips to two different parts of the material. If the bulb lights up then this shows that the material is a conductor. If the bulb does not light up then it is an insulator.

Imagine that you are using this circuit. Which materials do you **as a group** think will act as an insulator and which will act as a conductor?

Make sure you find out what each person in your group thinks. Talk about your reasons. Make sure you come to an agreed **group** prediction and reason why you think the item will act as a conductor or an insulator.

1   We predict that a wooden chopstick will act as a conductor/insulator because

....

....

2   We predict that a flat metal pencil case will act as a conductor/insulator because

....

....

3   We predict that a plastic comb will act as a conductor/insulator because

....

....

4   We predict that a rubber band will act as a conductor/insulator because

....

....

5   We predict that water in a glass will act as a conductor/insulator because

....

....

Unit 13

Planning group work

Resources

Worksheet 13a, pens, paper and materials for the 'Great gadgets' task.

Learning objectives

- To get pupils thinking about how they can plan and organise themselves and their work during group-work tasks so that they are less reliant on the teacher.
- To give pupils practice in planning and organising their group work during different types of task.

Briefing – whole-class work (ten minutes)

Explain to pupils that they have been doing quite a lot of group work but that you have often been deciding how the group work should be done, how they should organise themselves and so on. Discuss the above objectives. Explain that they are now going to think together about how they can plan and organise *their own* group work.

Either in the context of an imaginary piece of group work or in terms of preparation for the 'Great gadgets' task, discuss the things pupils will have to think about when planning and organising their own group work so that they can come up with a plan of action. What will they have to think about to prepare for this task? How can they make sure that everyone is involved and contributing efficiently?

Some things to consider doing when planning for group work:

- Timetabling – How can they use their time effectively? How much time should they spend doing different jobs? Do they need to evaluate how things are going so that they can change their plan if need be?
- Group roles – Are group roles needed? If so, which ones? (Refer to roles outlined on p. 110.)
- Brainstorming – Will the group need to brainstorm ideas? Will people need some individual thinking time to develop some ideas?
- Decision making – Will the group need to make *joint* decisions?
- Sub-tasks – Can the main task be broken down into smaller tasks? If so, can any of these be done at the same time?
- Sub-groups – For which tasks will the group need to work together to make joint decisions? Can the group split up to do some specific jobs?
- Note-taking/recording – Will a record or minutes be needed?

Briefing – whole-class work (five minutes)

Discuss the main objectives for the lesson. Remind pupils about what they did in the last lesson and pick up on some of the ways they went about planning for their paired work. Build a discussion on this and how they could take it forward.

Group work – 'Great gadgets' (twenty minutes)

The idea behind this task is to create an unrealistic time pressure, which will persuade groups to break into sub-groups, delegate jobs, identify roles for different sub-tasks and co-ordinate these sub-groups and sub-tasks.

Split the class into groups of five or six pupils. Outline what they will have to do in the main part of the activity but do not give them any materials to work with. Groups should be given five minutes to plan how they will do their group-work activity and to anticipate any problems. You may then want to have a whole-class discussion in which groups outline how they will be organising their group work and possibly adjust their plans.

Groups are to devise a 'great gadget' (see Worksheet 13a) with a catchy name, a billboard poster and a TV commercial to advertise it, possibly featuring a short poem or a jingle. They will have only *fifteen minutes* (or an even less realistic deadline) to complete this task. Give the groups the materials they need to do their tasks:

- Card, paper clips, elastic bands, lolly sticks or pencils, etc. – to build the gadget.
- Paper and one pen – to design the billboard poster.
- Paper and one pen – to write the TV advert.

Remind groups to pay special attention to the practicality, usefulness, sleekness of design, and saleability of the gadget. Their gadget will be judged on these criteria by the rest of the class, who will see the gadget, poster and TV advert at the end of the task.

Do not remind pupils that their time is nearly up until they have only a minute to go, since this is the job of a time-keeper. If they run out of time, they could finish their gadgets, posters or adverts at a later point.

Having seen each group's gadget, billboard poster and TV advert, the other groups should provide feedback (positive and negative) and/or rate the work: for example, thumbs up or down from each group on criteria such as practicality, usefulness, sleekness of design, saleability, to find out which gadget people are most likely to buy.

Debriefing (ten to fifteen minutes)

Discuss with the class how the groups organised their work, possibly using the following questions:

- How did you plan your group work?
- How could you have organised things better?
- Did you use roles?
- Was this helpful and why?
- Could you have performed your role better?
- Did anyone feel they had nothing or little to do?
- How did your group decide what type of gadget to make?
- Did every group member have an opportunity to express an idea or view?
- Did any group split into smaller groups that were given particular jobs?
- Did this work well?
- Did anyone experience a breakdown in co-ordination between the sub-groups?
- Did any group have any disagreements?
- How did they resolve problems given that there was so little time?

Follow-up work

You may like to set longer-term projects which can be carried out over a few sessions or weeks and involve a number of sub tasks. Encourage groups to plan their group work actively beforehand and to review progress at regular intervals.

Worksheet 13a: Great gadgets

Your group task is going to be to devise a 'great gadget' that can be used in the kitchen, at school, on a building site, in a hospital or anywhere you want. It has to be useful and practical, look good and people must want to buy it. You will also need to create a billboard poster such as you see on the side of roads and an idea for a TV advert with a short poem or jingle to promote your great gadget. Your gadget must have a catchy name.

   You will have only a short amount of time to do this task, so you will need to plan how you are going to do the group work. You may not have enough time to do all of the work together. Here are some questions to help you in your planning.

- Will you need to do some brainstorming?

- What decisions will have to be agreed by the whole group?

- Will you need to have group-work roles? Why? Which ones will you need?

- Will you need to split the group into smaller groups to do different parts of the task?

- Do you need to have a timetable?

What is your plan of action?

First we are going to ....

....

Then we will ....

....

Then ....

....

Then ....

....

Then ....

....

Then ....

....

- How many minutes will you spend on each task?
- What problems do you think may arise?
- How will you deal with them?

Contributors

The background research and writing of *Promoting Effective Group Work in the Classroom* was made possible by the collaborative actions of many researchers, teachers, pupils and schools. The authorship of this handbook identifies only the main researchers of the SPRinG project (see Chapter 1) at Key Stages 1 and 2. The ordering of the collaborating authors denotes varying responsibilities in the development, implementation and writing up of the material in the handbook.

Main authors

The names of the main authors are presented alphabetically. This was a truly collaborative effort over many years of working together on various research and education projects.

Ed Baines was the principal research officer of the Key Stage 2 component of the SPRinG project and was instrumental in the development of the research. He took a lead role in the conceptualisation and preparation of this handbook, working collaboratively with colleagues and teachers to develop the recommended practices and training activities. He is an experienced researcher in this field, working on a range of projects on peer relations in school (funded by the ESRC, Nuffield Foundation, Spencer Foundation and others).

Peter Blatchford co-directed the SPRinG project and maintained responsibility for the administration of the project in general and the Key Stage 2 developments in particular. Working with Peter Kutnick and Ed Baines, he developed and co-directed projects concerned with social pedagogy and the use of pupil groupings in classrooms that formed the basis of the SPRinG project and the theoretical underpinning of the main principles of effective group working. He has also carried out extensive research on class size and the deployment and impact of support staff in schools, as well as breaktime and peer relations in schools.

Peter Kutnick co-directed the SPRinG project and maintained responsibility for the Key Stage 1 developments. He has a long history of research and has published widely in this area. In addition to working with colleagues on the development of social pedagogy and the use of pupil groups, he was responsible for the development of the 'relational approach' that underlies effective grouping and interaction among children as well as co-developing theories and principles that underlie effective group working in pre-schools, primary and secondary schools.

Collaborating researchers

Anne Chowne is a teacher trainer who helped develop the Key Stage 2 ideas and activities with teachers and supported the implementation and evaluation of the SPR*in*G approach with Key Stage 2 teachers.

Cathy Ota and **Lucia Berdondini** were responsible for the co-development of Key Stage 1 activities and the initial structuring of material for the handbook. In particular, they worked with teachers to refine and implement the 'relational approach' and support systems for Key Stage 1 teachers, and they are responsible for the training organisation Working with Others.

Index